WASHINGTON NATIONALS

IQ

TUCKER ELLIOT

ISBN: 978-0-9912699-8-3

Special thanks to Dan "One Win" Monfre.

Front cover photo courtesy of Mark Whitt.

Interior layout and formatting by BMP Digital.

Black Mesa

Florida

CONTENTS

For Jessica, Sophie, and Charlie
Extraordinary teacher and friend
All diehard fans

INTRODUCTION

Arthur Daley, the Pulitzer Prize-winning sportswriter for the *New York Times*, wrote more than eleven thousand daily columns and twenty million words covering sports all over the world—but his favorite sport was baseball, and on that subject he famously wrote, "A baseball fan has the digestive apparatus of a billy goat. He can, and does, devour any set of statistics with insatiable appetite and then nuzzles hungrily for more."

Daley was right, of course.

Baseball relies on numbers and statistics more than any other sport—and we use those numbers to measure success and failure, they guide our decisions in playing and managing the game, they fuel our discussions when watching the game as a spectator or reliving it over the water cooler at work, and they keep us awake late at night, celebrating or lamenting, depending on, well, the final score.

Numbers, for the most part, don't lie.

Statistics on the other hand … well, it depends who you ask.

Bob Woolf was a Boston lawyer and a pioneer in the business of representing athletes in contract negotiations and sponsorship deals. In other words, he was one of the first sports agents. Woolf related this anecdote about Boston Red Sox pitcher Bob Stanley: "When I negotiated his contract with the Red Sox, we had statistics demonstrating he was the third best pitcher in the league. They had a chart showing he was the sixtieth best pitcher in the Red Sox organization." Perhaps it's the ability to manipulate and interpret statistics that makes numbers so fascinating to baseball fans.

Here's what I know about baseball and numbers that is incontrovertible: Math was my favorite grade school subject because it was the easiest. I knew it already from calculating batting averages and earned run averages and projecting how many hits and RBIs I'd have at the end of the season based on the games I'd already played—math skills that were easily three or four years ahead of my grade level at the time. My mom was the official scorekeeper at our Little League games and we'd spend hours each week pouring through the scorebook, tabulating all the stats, and then placing them in columns and charts on construction paper as if it was the back of my very own Topps baseball card.

Numbers resonate with baseball fans, no question about it.

It's not just the stats, either. We use numbers to track the performance of our favorite players, sure, but we also use numbers to identify them—as in jersey numbers. I met Johnny Bench once during spring training. Big surprise—I wore #5 a few weeks later when my summer league kicked off. You can track my idols using my Little League and high school jersey numbers: #5 (Bench), #8 (Gary Carter), #23 (Don Mattingly), and #8 again (Cal Ripken Jr.). There's a very good reason why franchises retire jersey numbers to honor their most important stars—just as a fan wearing a #22 Nationals jersey is making a statement about Juan Soto's contributions to the club, when the club retires a number it's making a statement about that player's significance to the history of the entire organization.

This is a book of trivia, but it is derived from numbers.

And collectively they tell the story of the Washington Nationals.

Now step up to the plate.

Challenge yourself.

Enjoy, and reminisce.

This is your Washington Nationals IQ, the ultimate test of true fandom.

"Thank you for all the dough. That really helped."

— *Mike Rizzo, speaking to the Lerner family, after the Nationals signed Stephen Strasburg to a seven-year, $175 million extension*

1 THE NUMBERS GAME

Any self-respecting fan should be able to cite the most notable and historic stats in franchise history—and you should also be able to identify the most revered jersey numbers as well. Nationals history is replete with superstars and individuals who distinguished themselves as fan-favorites, and that's why we open the top of the first with a simple numbers game: Do you know the jersey numbers for these all-time greats?

TOP OF THE FIRST

Q1: Gary Carter was an All-Star and runner-up in Rookie of the Year balloting as a 21-year-old kid in 1975. He split time between catching and playing the outfield that first year, but in 1976 he won the full-time job behind the plate. Carter was enshrined into the Hall of Fame in 2003. What is the jersey number retired by the Nationals/Expos in his honor?

    a) 3
    b) 8
    c) 13
    d) 18

Q2: Tim Raines was an All-Star and runner-up in Rookie of the Year balloting as a 21-year-old kid in 1981. He led the league with 71 stolen bases as a rookie and kept his foot on the gas pedal for the next two decades. He was finally enshrined at Cooperstown in 2017. What is the jersey number retired by the Nationals/Expos in his honor?

    a) 10
    b) 20
    c) 30
    d) 40

Q3: Andre Dawson won six consecutive Gold Glove Awards for the Expos and placed second in MVP balloting twice (1981, 1983). He's also one of just five players in franchise history with 200 home runs and 700 RBIs. Dawson was inducted into the Hall of Fame in 2010. What is the jersey number retired by the Nationals/Expos in his honor?

    a) 8

b) 10

c) 12

d) 15

Q4: Rusty Staub was the very first All-Star in franchise history. Staub was 25 years old when the Expos acquired him via trade prior to their inaugural 1969 season, but Staub was already a six-year veteran. He made an immediate impact on the club and became a fan-favorite affectionately referred to as "Le Grand Orange" for his red hair. What is the jersey number retired by the Nationals/Expos in his honor?

a) 10

b) 20

c) 30

d) 40

Q5: Steve Rogers was runner-up in 1973 Rookie of the Year balloting after posting 10 wins against five losses as a 23-year-old rookie. He would play every one of his 13 big-league seasons with the Montreal Expos and was a five-time All-Star. What jersey number did Steve Rogers wear for the Montreal Expos?

a) 15

b) 25

c) 35

d) 45

Q6: Tim Wallach won the Golden Spikes Award as the best amateur player in the country in 1979—the same season he led Cal State Fullerton to victory in the College World Series. Wallach was the Expos first-round draft pick that same year, and a few weeks later, in the first at-bat of his professional career, he homered for the Memphis Chicks. Wallach was a five-time All-Star during 11 full seasons as the everyday third baseman. What jersey number did Tim

Wallach wear for the Montreal Expos?

  a) 27
  b) 29
  c) 37
  d) 39

Q7: The Montreal Expos signed Vladimir Guerrero after an open tryout in the Dominican Republic. It took only a few BP swings for scout Arturo DeFreites to offer him a contract. A year later he was the *Sporting News* Minor League Player of the Year, and a year after that he debuted in a critical September series vs. the Atlanta Braves as the Expos were fighting for a berth in the playoffs. What jersey number did Hall of Famer Vladimir Guerrero wear for the Montreal Expos?

  a) 7
  b) 17
  c) 27
  d) 37

Q8: Canadian-born Larry Walker hit 19 home runs as a rookie in 1989. That tied Andre Dawson for the most rookie home runs in Expos history. Walker would go on to be a perennial MVP candidate while winning numerous Gold Glove and Silver Slugger Awards. Walker was inducted into the Canadian Sports Hall of Fame in 2007 and the Canadian Baseball Hall of Fame in 2009. What jersey number did Larry Walker wear for the Montreal Expos?

  a) 3
  b) 13
  c) 23
  d) 33

Q9: Dennis Martinez was the first Nicaraguan-born player in major-league history. He spent the first years of his career in Baltimore, but later signed a free agent contract to play for the Expos. Good move for the club. Martinez—affectionately dubbed "El Presidente"—was a three-time All-Star and won 100 games over eight seasons. What jersey number did Dennis Martinez wear for the Montreal Expos?

a) 12
b) 21
c) 23
d) 32

Q10: Montreal acquired Hall of Famer Pedro Martinez after his rookie season with the Los Angeles Dodgers in exchange for Delino DeShields. All he did from 1994-97 was win 55 games against 33 losses. He had 20 complete games, eight shutouts, and a 3.06 ERA—all were the best on the club during his tenure in Montreal. What jersey number did Pedro Martinez wear for the Montreal Expos?

a) 42
b) 43
c) 44
d) 45

TOP OF THE FIRST ANSWER KEY

1: b. 8.

2: c. 30.

3: b. 10.

4: a. 10.

5: d. 45.

6: b. 29.

7: c. 27.

8: d. 33.

9: d. 32.

10: d. 45.

BOTTOM OF THE FIRST

Q11: Ryan Zimmerman was the fourth overall pick in 2005 out of the University of Virginia—and the very first draft pick in Nationals history. Less than three months later he made his big-league debut. Zimmerman—who was runner-up in Rookie of the Year balloting in 2006—would go on to play more games for the Nationals than any player in history. He wore #25 on his jersey during his 2005 call-up ... but what jersey number did Ryan Zimmerman wear for the Washington Nationals from 2006-19?

    a) 11
    b) 21
    c) 31
    d) 41

Q12: Stephen Strasburg was the overall #1 pick in the 2009 draft—and when he debuted in 2010, his starts were the biggest attendance draw in the game. Home or away, fans came out in record numbers to see his fastball. Well, to hear the pop of the catcher's mitt, at least. He was 5-3 in 12 starts with an astounding 92 strikeouts in just 68 innings when his season was cut short by a tear in the ulnar collateral ligament of his right elbow. He was back on the mound by the end of 2011, and has since been one of the game's best pitchers. What jersey number did Stephen Strasburg wear for the Washington Nationals?

    a) 17
    b) 27
    c) 37
    d) 47

Q13: Max Scherzer was a first-round draft pick of the Arizona Diamondbacks in 2006. He made his big-league debut two years later, and two years after that he was on the path to superstardom in Detroit. The Nats signed him as a free agent in 2015 and he's been worth every penny. In five seasons from 2015-19, Scherzer won more games (79), pitched more innings (1,050 2/3), and struck out more batters (1,371) than any other pitcher in the NL. What jersey number did Max Scherzer wear for the Washington Nationals?

a) 31
b) 33
c) 35
d) 37

Q14: Bryce Harper might be the most heralded high school player in history. Harper, who was the first-ever underclassman to win the Baseball America High School Player of the Year Award, was so dominant at Las Vegas High School that he left after his sophomore year and enrolled at the Community College of Southern Nevada in search of better competition. A 502-foot home run at Tropicana Field and an appearance on the cover of *Sports Illustrated*—when he was 17 years old—cemented his status. The Nats made him the first overall pick in the 2010 draft and just two years later he was the National League Rookie of the Year. What jersey number did Bryce Harper wear for the Washington Nationals?

a) 14
b) 24
c) 34
d) 44

Q15: Jordan Zimmermann was a second-round draft pick out of the University of Wisconsin at Stevens Point in 2007. Just two years later he debuted for the Nationals—and by 2011 he was a permanent fixture in the rotation. In fact, from 2011-15 no pitcher won as many games (66) or pitched as many innings (971 2/3) for the Nationals as did Zimmermann. What jersey number did Jordan Zimmermann wear for the Washington Nationals?

    a) 27

    b) 28

    c) 29

    d) 30

Q16: Jayson Werth signed with the Nationals as a free agent after four successful seasons and a World Series title with the Philadelphia Phillies. He was a key component of the Nationals offense for the next seven years with 109 home runs, 781 hits, 393 RBIs, and 450 runs—all of which rank among the top-three on the club during his tenure. What jersey number did Jayson Werth wear for the Washington Nationals?

    a) 13

    b) 28

    c) 42

    d) 54

Q17: The Nationals acquired lefty Gio Gonzalez in a trade prior to the 2012 season. In seven seasons (2012-18), Gonzalez won 86 games with a 3.62 ERA. Only Stephen Strasburg won more games (88) for the Nationals during that time period. What jersey number did Gio Gonzalez wear for the Washington Nationals?

    a) 43

    b) 45

    c) 47

    d) 49

Q18: From 2012-14, no Nationals player had more home runs (79) or RBIs (254) than did Adam LaRoche. The son of a big-league pitcher, LaRoche won a Gold Glove Award and a Silver Slugger Award while playing first base for two division-winning Nats teams. What jersey number did Adam LaRoche wear for the Washington Nationals?

a) 5
b) 15
c) 25
d) 35

Q19: The New York Mets selected Hubie Brooks as the overall #3 pick of the 1978 draft. A talented all-around player, his versatility made him invaluable when he arrived in Montreal via trade in 1985. Sabermetrics guru Bill James said this of Brooks: "He was a lot more valuable in reality than on paper; every team has a hole somewhere, and Brooks was a player who could fill that hole and not hurt you in the process." What jersey number did Hubie Brooks wear during five seasons with the Montreal Expos?

a) 7
b) 21
c) 30
d) 39

Q20: Andres Galarraga debuted with the Expos in 1985 and a year later won starting duties at first base. "The Big Cat" played eight seasons and 951 games for Montreal, and ranks among the franchise leaders in slugging, runs, hits, total bases, doubles, home runs, and RBIs. What was his primary jersey number with the Montreal Expos?

a) 2
b) 14
c) 22
d) 24

BOTTOM OF THE FIRST ANSWER KEY

11: a. 11.

12: c. 37.

13: a. 31.

14: c. 34.

15: a. 27.

16: b. 28.

17: c. 47.

18: c. 25.

19: a. 7.

20: b. 14.

"That's a clown question, bro'."

— *Bryce Harper*

2 BASEBALL QUOTES

No other sport inspires quotes like baseball. Dozens of books are out there filled with nothing but quotes from the game's great players, managers, umpires, writers, and broadcasters. One reason we're fascinated with baseball quotes is because they tell us the history of the game in the words of those who were there to make or witness firsthand the plays that inspired generations of fans. And lucky for us, baseball has inspired more written words than any other sport.

Here in the second our trivia is inspired by our love for baseball quotes. Do you know which players these words were spoken about?

TOP OF THE SECOND

Q21: Sportscaster and former pitcher Ron Darling said of this player: "If it's round and has got some stitching on it, he's swinging."
a) Andre Dawson
b) Gary Carter
c) Vladimir Guerrero
d) Ryan Zimmerman

Q22: Nationals general manager Mike Rizzo said of this player: "He is the epitome of a lead-by-example guy. If I said it once, I said it a million times to the other younger players: 'Just watch the way he prepares.'"
a) Adam LaRoche
b) Ryan Zimmerman
c) Ian Desmond
d) Daniel Murphy

Q23: Hall of Fame legend Tony Gwynn managed this pitcher at San Diego State University—but Gwynn didn't let him bat. Now fast-forward to this pitcher's professional debut with the AA Harrisburg Senators. In that game he hit an RBI double, which prompted him to joke afterward: "I'm going to call Tony Gwynn up tomorrow and let him have it."
a) Gio Gonzalez
b) Max Scherzer
c) Stephen Strasburg
d) Jordan Zimmerman

Q24: *Los Angeles Times* writer Chuck Schilken said of this player: "... he just gave the guy a look that could kill and then delivered what is sure to be the catchphrase of the year."

   a) Jayson Werth

   b) Bryce Harper

   c) Stephen Strasburg

   d) Jordan Zimmermann

Q25: Longtime big-league manager Chuck Tanner once said of this player: "He's not a good player. He's a great one."

   a) Larry Walker

   b) Andre Dawson

   c) Tim Raines

   d) Vladimir Guerrero

Q26: Upon his selection to the Canadian Baseball Hall of Fame in 2014, this player said: "I'm honored … what a great thrill … to join many of my old teammates and manager, along with so many people that meant so much to Canadian baseball. This is a great honor for my family and myself."

   a) Tim Wallach

   b) Tim Raines

   c) Andre Dawson

   d) Pedro Martinez

Q27: Hall of Famer Ryne Sandberg once said of this player: "No player in baseball history worked harder, suffered more or did better than [him]. He's the best I've ever seen."

   a) Gary Carter

   b) Andre Dawson

   c) Vladimir Guerrero

   d) Tim Raines

Q28: Hall of Famer Randy Johnson said of this player: "[He's] the first person I've ever seen with an above-average fastball and an above-average change-up."

a) Pedro Martinez

b) Stephen Strasburg

c) Jordan Zimmermann

d) Max Scherzer

Q29: This productive hitter and fan-favorite had a simple philosophy that endeared him to Nationals fans: "I like to be aggressive out there, sometimes to a fault. But you play hard and play the game the right way."

a) Bryce Harper

b) Adam Dunn

c) Adam LaRoche

d) Jayson Werth

Q30: Former player Sean Casey said of this powerful slugger: "[He's] one of those special talents who comes around once every twenty years … someone who really changes a game and can hit the ball as far as anybody in the league."

a) Bryce Harper

b) Adam Dunn

c) Adam LaRoche

d) Jayson Werth

TOP OF THE SECOND ANSWER KEY

21: c. Vladimir Guerrero.

22: b. Ryan Zimmerman.

23: c. Stephen Strasburg.

24: b. Bryce Harper ("That's a clown question, bro'").

25: c. Tim Raines.

26: a. Tim Wallach.

27: b. Andre Dawson.

28: a. Pedro Martinez.

29: d. Jayson Werth.

30: b. Adam Dunn.

BOTTOM OF THE SECOND

Q31: Nationals hitting coach Kevin Long gave a pithy reply when asked about this player: "He smashes fastballs."
  a) Anthony Rendon
  b) Daniel Murphy
  c) Juan Soto
  d) Bryce Harper

Q32: Daniel Murphy made the case to fans for why this teammate should be included on the All-Star roster: "Do you go to FanGraphs?"
  a) Anthony Rendon
  b) Trea Turner
  c) Juan Soto
  d) Bryce Harper

Q33: This manager described his decision-making process as: "I don't know why I do stuff sometimes. Sometimes I go by the numbers. Sometimes I go on what I feel. Sometimes I go on what I hope."
  a) Davey Johnson
  b) Matt Williams
  c) Dusty Baker
  d) Dave Martinez

Q34: In a postgame press conference, this Nationals pitcher said: "Strikeouts are sexy."
  a) Jordan Zimmermann
  b) Stephen Strasburg
  c) Max Scherzer

d) Tanner Roark

Q35: This pitcher hit a home run and tossed a two-hit gem over six shutout innings vs. the Marlins ... but it's what he said *after* the game to MASN broadcaster Bob Carpenter that got everyone's attention. Carpenter asked how the pitcher dealt with difficult cold weather conditions. The reply: "It was tough to get a grip. I felt like I was making love to my hand."
  a) Max Scherzer
  b) Tanner Roark
  c) Gio Gonzalez
  d) Doug Fister

Q36: This player walked three times during his big-league debut, which prompted Giants first baseman Will Clark to tell him: "It's your first game ... and they're pitching you like you're Babe Ruth."
  a) Vladimir Guerrero
  b) Larry Walker
  c) Andres Galarraga
  d) Rondell White

Q37: This player earned the nickname "The Kid" for his enthusiasm and hustle during his first invite to spring training. He would later say, "I tried to impress everybody that spring, you know, being the first in line for sprints. Running hard to first base all the time." Who was "The Kid"?
  a) Andre Dawson
  b) Tim Raines
  c) Gary Carter
  d) Larry Walker

Q38: Baseball columnist Jayson Stark once wrote about this

notoriously deliberate pitcher: "Man, he works slow. I swear a gentleman sitting behind me read half of *War and Peace* while he was out there."

    a) Javier Vazquez

    b) Jordan Zimmermann

    c) John Lannan

    d) Livan Hernandez

Q39: This player got his start on an inner-city street with the help of a youth coach—and post-baseball career he began a foundation to do the same for others. He said: "I got so much out of my youth coaches and what they taught me at an early age really made a difference. When I was young, I didn't have a ride to practice, I didn't have equipment, I didn't have much at all, but those coaches were there for me and made a real impact on my life."

    a) Pedro Martinez

    b) Larry Walker

    c) Rondell White

    d) Marquis Grissom

Q40: This player said: "When I hit the ball, I do want to hurt it."

    a) Alfonso Soriano

    b) Vladimir Guerrero

    c) Bryce Harper

    d) Adam Dunn

BOTTOM OF THE SECOND ANSWER KEY

31: c. Juan Soto.

32: a. Anthony Rendon.

33: c. Dusty Baker.

34: c. Max Scherzer.

35: c. Gio Gonzalez.

36: b. Larry Walker.

37: c. Gary Carter.

38: d. Livan Hernandez.

39: d. Marquis Grissom.

40: c. Bryce Harper.

"It's hard to think about things like that when you're still playing. But it's not too bad for a guy who's supposed to be a defensive specialist."

— Ryan Zimmerman, after his 200th career home run

3 FRANCHISE RECORDS

The story of baseball in Washington has its origins on a sandlot just south of the White House that dates to the mid-1800s. Washington's inaugural professional franchise—also the Nationals—joined the National League in 1886, but ironically was contracted when the league reduced its teams from 12 to eight in 1900. In the century that followed the Washington Senators joined the American League and won a World Series title in 1924—but that club eventually relocated to Minnesota and became the Twins in 1961. A second iteration of the Washington Senators began play in D.C. that same year—but that club never made the playoffs until after it relocated to Texas and became the Rangers in 1972.

Meanwhile, Major League Baseball's first non-American franchise began play in 1969—the Montreal Expos.

The Expos always had talent, but found their way to the playoffs just once. Bad business decisions, fiscal uncertainty, and poor attendance plagued the club for three decades. The nail in the coffin was the 1994 players' strike. Commissioner Bud Selig threatened contraction but eventually a deal to relocate to D.C. was negotiated. The *story* of D.C. baseball begins more than 150 years ago—but the *origin* of today's Nationals is north of the border and includes Hall of Fame legends Gary Carter, Tim Raines, Andre Dawson, Vladimir Guerrero, and Pedro Martinez. It's important to celebrate the players who've made today's club one of the most talented in the game—but it would be wrong to dismiss the achievements of the guys who toiled in near anonymity with the Expos.

Here in the third, we explore some of the most significant franchise records and relive moments from some of the biggest names in the game.

For clarity purposes, "franchise record" refers to 1969 to the present and includes stats from both the Expos and the Nationals. "Expos record" and "Nationals record" are used to denote achievements specific to those eras of team history.

TOP OF THE THIRD

Q41: Tim Raines spent parts of 23 seasons playing major-league baseball from 1979-2002, and he retired as the most successful base stealer in history when ranked by percentage (84.7). What is the major-league record number of consecutive seasons that Tim Raines stole 70 or more bases?

    a) 5

    b) 6

    c) 7

    d) 8

Q42: This pitcher began his career in record form. In his first 14 big-league starts, his ERA was a miniscule 1.31. In major-league history the only number even close to that was 1.67 by Tiny Bonham for the 1940 New York Yankees. Who is this outstanding pitcher?

    a) Joe Hesketh

    b) Ugueth Urbina

    c) David Palmer

    d) Steve Rogers

Q43: Through 2019, there have been 16 different players in franchise history with at least one 100-RBI season ... but in that time, only one player had 100 RBIs as a rookie. Who is this slugger?

    a) Ryan Zimmerman

    b) Bryce Harper

    c) Larry Parrish

    d) Andre Dawson

Q44: The longest hitting streak in franchise history is 31 games. And nothing about it was cheap, either. This player had 24 extra-base hits—including 11 home runs—to go along with 26 runs and 27 RBIs during his streak. Who achieved this extraordinary record?

a) Andre Dawson

b) Warren Cromartie

c) David Segui

d) Vladimir Guerrero

Q45: And a follow-up … the longest hitting streak in Washington Nationals history is 30 games. Same thing, nothing cheap about it. This player had 19 extra-base hits—including eight home runs—to go along with 26 runs and 26 RBIs. Who holds this Nationals record?

a) Bryce Harper

b) Ryan Zimmerman

c) Brad Wilkerson

d) Nick Johnson

Q46: In 35 at-bats over 11 games, this player had 18 hits, seven doubles, and seven home runs … including a franchise record 11-game streak with at least one extra-base hit. Who achieved this phenomenal feat?

a) Bob Bailey

b) Warren Cromartie

c) Vladimir Guerrero

d) Fernando Tatis

Q47: And a follow-up … this player was the first in Nationals history to collect an extra-base hit in nine consecutive games. In 37 at-bats, he had 19 hits, four doubles, six home runs, 13 runs scored, and 16 RBIs. Who achieved this remarkable streak?

a) Bryce Harper

b) Ryan Zimmerman

c) Brad Wilkerson

d) Nick Johnson

Q48: The franchise record for consecutive games with a home run is four. Through 2019, it's been achieved 13 times by 11 different players. The first was Bob Bailey in 1970. Who was the most recent Nationals player to homer in four consecutive games?

a) Bryce Harper

b) Adam LaRoche

c) Mike Morse

d) Ryan Zimmerman

Q49: And a follow-up … four players in franchise history had six home runs during their four-game homer streaks. However, one Nats player actually hit six home runs in only three games. Who is the only player in franchise history with six home runs in just three games?

a) Bryce Harper

b) Adam LaRoche

c) Mike Morse

d) Ryan Zimmerman

Q50: Through 2019, seven players in franchise history scored at least one run in 10 consecutive games. An eighth player did one better. Who scored in a franchise record 11 consecutive games?

a) Denard Span

b) Brad Wilkerson

c) Endy Chavez

d) Nick Johnson

TOP OF THE THIRD ANSWER KEY

41: b. 6.

42: d. Steve Rogers (1973).

43: a. Ryan Zimmerman (2006).

44: d. Vladimir Guerrero (1999).

45: b. Ryan Zimmerman (2009).

46: a. Bob Bailey (1970).

47: b. Ryan Zimmerman (2017).

48: a. Bryce Harper (2016).

49: a. Bryce Harper (2015).

50: d. Nick Johnson (2005).

BOTTOM OF THE THIRD

Q51: Through 2019, five players in franchise history had a streak of eight consecutive games with at least one RBI. One of those players had a second streak with at least one RBI in a franchise record nine consecutive games. Who is this record-setting slugger?

a) Bryce Harper

b) Ryan Zimmerman

c) Moises Alou

d) Larry Walker

Q52: Only eight players in franchise history played 1,000 games with the club. The record is 1,767. Who played more games for the franchise than any other player in history?

a) Tim Wallach

b) Ryan Zimmerman

c) Gary Carter

d) Warren Cromartie

Q53: Chris Nabholz (1990) and Steve Rogers (1973) are the only pitchers in franchise history to win as many as six games during their first 10 career starts. The Washington Nationals record for most wins during a pitcher's first 10 career starts is five. Which pitchers share this record?

a) Stephen Strasburg/Luis Atilano

b) Joe Ross/Joel Hanrahan

c) Mike O'Connor/J.D. Martin

d) Jordan Zimmermann/Craig Stammen

Q54: The physical toll of a life behind the dish is immense. It's why fewer than 30 catchers in baseball history (through 2019) have hit safely in 20 or more consecutive games. The franchise record is 22. The numbers are ridiculously impressive: 25 for 78, with five doubles, five home runs, and 18 RBIs. Who achieved this extraordinary feat?

    a) Brian Schneider

    b) Wilson Ramos

    c) Gary Carter

    d) Ivan Rodriguez

Q55: This pitcher set a franchise record with 26 consecutive saves in a single-season. In 26 innings of work he struck out 22 batters but gave up just 18 hits, five walks, and three earned runs. By season's end he saved a league-best and franchise record 47 games. Who is this All-Star closer?

    a) Mel Rojas

    b) Jeff Reardon

    c) Rafael Soriano

    d) Chad Cordero

Q56: In franchise history, only 11 times has a player collected 100-plus hits at home in a single-season. Through 2019, the record is an astounding 113 hits in just 77 home games. Who holds this record?

    a) Vladimir Guerrero

    b) Jose Vidro

    c) Dave Cash

    d) Ryan Zimmerman

Q57: Through 2019, the Washington Nationals record for most home hits in a season is 108 in just 76 games. Who holds this record?

    a) Denard Span

    b) Ryan Zimmerman

    c) Alfonso Soriano

d) Anthony Rendon

Q58: This pitcher had a three-month stretch in which he logged 102 innings and 134 strikeouts with an earned run average of 2.10. His record was 12-0, but even more impressive was the fact the club won a franchise record 15 consecutive games with him on the mound. Who is this pitcher?

    a) Jordan Zimmermann

    b) Max Scherzer

    c) Stephen Strasburg

    d) Dennis Martinez

Q59: In the last 100 years of major-league history, approximately 80 games featured a player who made five plate appearances without recording an official at-bat. Walks, mostly. And a lot of them. Only three major-league players had a game with six plate appearances and no official at-bats: Miller Huggins (1910), Billy Urbanski (1934), and Jimmie Foxx (1938). There's only been one instance of a player with seven plate appearances and no official at-bats—and he did it for the Nationals. Who holds this major-league record?

    a) Ryan Zimmerman

    b) Anthony Rendon

    c) Bryce Harper

    d) Daniel Murphy

Q60: Tim Wallach hit 360 career doubles for the Expos. That total was the franchise record for a lot of years until Ryan Zimmerman finally surpassed it. Zimmerman closed out 2019 with 401 career two-baggers. But who holds the franchise season record with an impressive 54 doubles?

    a) Tim Wallach

    b) Ryan Zimmerman

c) Orlando Cabrera
d) Mark Grudzielanek

BOTTOM OF THE THIRD ANSWER KEY

51: b. Ryan Zimmerman.

52: a. Tim Wallach (through 2019, Ryan Zimmerman is at 1,689).

53: a. Stephen Strasburg (2010)/Luis Atilano (2010).

54: c. Gary Carter (1982).

55: d. Chad Cordero (2005).

56: b. Jose Vidro (2000).

57: a. Denard Span (2014).

58: c. Stephen Strasburg (2015-16).

59: c. Bryce Harper (2016).

60: d. Mark Grudzielanek (1997).

"Get to the playoffs and you've got a puncher's chance."

— *Mike Rizzo*

4 OCTOBER BASEBALL

"Next year" is the mentality that 29 of baseball's 30 teams cling to each winter, for there can be only one winner—as the 2012, 2014, 2016, and 2017 Nationals are painfully aware.

In the spring, the wins column is reset.

Last season is history.

And the goal is the same for every club: October baseball.

The journey is 162 games long, and the destination is a chance for baseball immortality. Let's take a look at the Nationals in the playoffs.

TOP OF THE FOURTH

Q61: This player hit one of the most dramatic and important home runs in Nationals history. It was a walk-off blast to force a decisive Game 5 in the 2012 NLDS vs. St. Louis. Which slugger gave fans an extraordinary October moment with one swing of the bat?

    a) Bryce Harper

    b) Ryan Zimmerman

    c) Mike Morse

    d) Jayson Werth

Q62: Ryan Zimmerman—the first-ever draft pick in Nationals history—closed out 2019 as a World Series champion and the franchise leader with 35 career postseason games played. However, from 2012—Washington's first-ever playoff team—through 2019, which player had the most postseason hits for the Nationals?

    a) Ryan Zimmerman

    b) Jayson Werth

    c) Bryce Harper

    d) Anthony Rendon

Q63: Bryce Harper hit a Nationals record five home runs during four trips to the postseason with the club. How many home runs did Juan Soto hit during his first-ever trip to the postseason in 2019?

    a) 2

    b) 3

    c) 4

    d) 5

Q64: The 1981 players' strike resulted in a split schedule with division winners declared for each half of the season. The Phillies won the season's first half title with a record of 34-21. The Expos won the second half title with a record of 30-23. Ironically, neither the Phillies nor the Expos had the best overall winning percentage in the division for the entire season ... which meant while the Phillies and Expos met in the Division Series, this team "won" the N.L. East but missed the playoffs. Which team lost a playoff berth to a players' strike?

    a) St. Louis Cardinals

    b) Pittsburgh Pirates

    c) New York Mets

    d) Chicago Cubs

Q65: The 1981 NLDS was a best-of-five series that began with the first-ever playoff game in franchise history on October 7 at Olympic Stadium. Steve Carlton was the starting (and losing) pitcher for the Phillies. Who was the starting (and winning) pitcher in that historic game for the Expos?

    a) Charlie Lea

    b) Ray Burris

    c) Bill Gullickson

    d) Steve Rogers

Q66: The first playoff hit in franchise history belongs to Warren Cromartie. He singled vs. Steve Carlton to start the bottom of the first inning. Gary Carter would pick up the first RBI when he doubled later that inning to give the Expos a 1-0 lead. Who scored on Carter's hit for the Expos' first-ever playoff run?

    a) Warren Cromartie

    b) Jerry White

    c) Andre Dawson

    d) Larry Parrish

Q67: The second game of the 1981 NLDS featured the first-ever playoff home run in franchise history. Whose two-run blast proved to be the difference as the Expos won 3-1 to take a two-game lead in the series vs. Philly?

    a) Gary Carter

    b) Tim Raines

    c) Andre Dawson

    d) Larry Parrish

Q68: The Phillies won Games 3 and 4 to force a decisive Game 5 in the 1981 NLDS. It was an afternoon game played on October 11 in front of 47,384 maniacal fans at Veterans Stadium in Philadelphia, but the moment belonged to Steve Rogers. He outdueled Steve Carlton, and gave up just six hits in a masterful performance. The result: 3-0, good guys. And a trip to the NLCS. Whose two-run fifth-inning single gave Rogers the only support he would need to lead the Expos to victory on that afternoon?

    a) Jerry White

    b) Terry Francona

    c) Jerry Manuel

    d) Steve Rogers

Q69: The Expos' opponent in the 1981 NLCS was the Los Angeles Dodgers. The Dodgers had experience, great pitching, and one of the more potent offenses in the league—and it would have been easy for the Expos to roll over after LA posted a decisive 5-1 victory in Game 1 of the series. Instead, this guy blanked LA 5-0 in Game 2 at Dodger Stadium. Whose five-hit shutout tied the best-of-five series at two games apiece?

    a) Elias Sosa

    b) Ray Burris

c) Bill Gullickson

d) Bill Lee

Q70: Steve Rogers took the mound to face the Dodgers and Jerry Reuss in the pivotal Game 3 match-up. Reuss held a 1-0 advantage until two outs in the sixth. A Larry Parrish single tied the game, and then this guy ... whose unlikely—*he hit only three in the regular season!*—three-run home run was the difference in Montreal's 4-1 victory?

a) Terry Francona

b) Jerry Manuel

c) Jerry White

d) Bobby Ramos

TOP OF THE FOURTH ANSWER KEY

61: d. Jayson Werth.

62: d. Anthony Rendon.

63: d. 5 (through 2019, Anthony Rendon, Ryan Zimmerman, Bryce Harper, and Juan Soto share the record for postseason home runs).

64: a. St. Louis Cardinals.

65: d. Steve Rogers.

66: b. Jerry White.

67: a. Gary Carter.

68: d. Steve Rogers.

69: b. Ray Burris.

70: c. Jerry White.

BOTTOM OF THE FOURTH

Q71: The 2012 National League Division Series was the first-ever playoff series for the Washington Nationals. It opened in St. Louis with 21-game winner Gio Gonzalez on the mound to face Adam Wainwright. Whose single in the second inning was the first playoff hit in Nationals history?

    a) Ryan Zimmerman

    b) Mike Morse

    c) Ian Desmond

    d) Danny Espinosa

Q72: The Nationals overcame seven walks by starter Gio Gonzalez and 10 strikeouts by opposing pitcher Adam Wainwright to win that first playoff game—but it took a two-out, two-run, bloop pinch-hit single off the bat of an unlikely hero to get the job done. The game's hero would later say: "I was just trying to calm myself down and try to make some things happen and not strike out." Whose eighth-inning heroics won the first playoff game in Nationals history?

    a) Roger Bernadina

    b) Chad Tracy

    c) Tyler Moore

    d) Wilson Ramos

Q73: Lance Lynn and the Cardinals dominated Jordan Zimmermann and the Nationals, 12-4, in Game 2 of that series. However, the Nationals did get their first-ever playoff home run. Whose fifth-inning blast made Nationals history?

    a) Jayson Werth

    b) Bryce Harper

    c) Adam LaRoche

d) Ryan Zimmerman

Q74: This Nationals star struggled through the early part of the 2012 playoffs. He was 1 for 10 with six strikeouts through two games … which explains this reply to a reporter's question: "Do I look overanxious? You think so? Maybe you should be a hitting coach." Whose snarky reply made headlines during the 2012 playoffs?
    a) Jayson Werth
    b) Adam LaRoche
    c) Mike Morse
    d) Bryce Harper

Q75: Washington's first venture into October ended disastrously. The Nationals led Game 5 of the 2012 NLDS 6-0 in the third inning. With nine outs to go the lead was 6-3. With three outs to go the lead was 7-5. After Carlos Beltran doubled to start the Cardinals' ninth against closer Drew Storen, Matt Holliday grounded out and Allen Craig struck out to move the Nationals within one out of advancing to the League Championship Series. Then, disaster: Back-to-back walks to Yadier Molina and David Freese loaded the bases, Daniel Descalso's single tied the game … and then this guy. Whose two-out, two-run single against Drew Storen capped the Cardinals' rally and ended the Nationals' season?
    a) Pete Kozma
    b) Shane Robinson
    c) Skip Schumaker
    d) Matt Carpenter

Q76: The bottom line is fandom is painful. It's a hard truth, and fans got a second lesson in just how hard it is after the Nats' return to the playoffs in 2014. The San Francisco Giants, with Jake Peavy on the mound, beat Stephen Strasburg, 3-2, in Game 1 of the NLDS. In

Game 2, Jordan Zimmermann blanked the Giants for 8 2/3 innings, held a 1-0 lead, and had retired 20 consecutive batters ... but he was removed by manager Matt Williams after he walked Joe Panik with two outs in the ninth. Williams would later say, "Why did we decide to take him out? Because if he got in trouble in the ninth or got a baserunner, we were going to bring our closer in. That is what we have done all year." Drew Storen came in and gave up a single to Buster Posey, which gave this guy a chance ... who hit a game-tying double and set the stage for the 18-inning marathon that followed?

a) Hunter Pence
b) Pablo Sandoval
c) Brandon Belt
d) Travis Ishikawa

Q77: And a follow-up ... the Nats' eighth reliever of the game was Tanner Roark. He was 27 years old when the game began. Some six hours later and past midnight the game ended with Roark the losing pitcher on his 28th birthday. Whose home run against Roark in the 18th inning gave the Giants a 2-1 victory in the longest playoff game in history?

a) Hunter Pence
b) Pablo Sandoval
c) Brandon Belt
d) Travis Ishikawa

Q78: And one more follow-up ... the offense managed just nine hits against Tim Hudson and seven relievers, but had just two hits over the final nine innings. The Giants' Yusmeiro Petit actually pitched six innings of one-hit relief with seven strikeouts. Which trio of Nationals' stars combined to go 0-for-21 in this heartbreaking loss?

a) Jayson Werth, Anthony Rendon, Ian Desmond

b) Denard Span, Adam LaRoche, Bryce Harper

c) Anthony Rendon, Denard Span, Bryce Harper

d) Adam LaRoche, Ian Desmond, Jayson Werth

Q79: In 2016, the Nationals had Max Scherzer on the mound for Game 5 of the NLDS vs. the Dodgers, and were just nine outs from advancing to the NLCS ... but a Joc Pederson home run knocked Scherzer from the game, and when the bullpen took over the floodgates opened. The Dodgers scored four times in the seventh and held on to win, 4-3. How many Nationals' relievers did it take to get three outs in the seventh inning?

   a) 2

   b) 3

   c) 4

   d) 5

Q80: In 2017, facing elimination in the Division Series yet again, Stephen Strasburg took the mound at Wrigley Field and held the Cubs to just three hits over seven dominant innings. Strasburg struck out 12. He later said, "I just focused on one pitch at a time and going as long as I could." The victory sent the series back to Washington for a decisive Game 5—and it included a bit of history on offense. Who hit the first postseason grand slam in Nationals history to secure the 5-0 victory?

   a) Trea Turner

   b) Jayson Werth

   c) Daniel Murphy

   d) Michael A. Taylor

BOTTOM OF THE FOURTH ANSWER KEY

71: c. Ian Desmond.

72: c. Tyler Moore.

73: d. Ryan Zimmerman.

74: d. Bryce Harper.

75: a. Pete Kozma.

76: b. Pablo Sandoval.

77: c. Brandon Belt.

78: b. Denard Span, Adam LaRoche, Bryce Harper.

79: d. 5.

80: d. Michael A. Taylor.

"When I hit the ball, I do want to hurt it."

— *Bryce Harper*

5 THE SLUGGERS

In the fifth, it's all about the sluggers. Guys who can hit *bombs*. One hit three home runs in one game … *three times*. Another homered on *five* different Opening Days. And yet another hit *11 walk-off bombs*.

Want home run titles?

Check.

Want bombs in the playoffs?

Check.

Bombs that set major-league records?

Check.

Record-setting bombs by rookies?

Check.

The list could go on, and on, and on.

Let's get started.

TOP OF THE FIFTH

Q81: This veteran won the first batting title—and two-thirds of the Triple Crown—in Montreal Expos history. He led the league in five categories: 204 hits, 43 doubles, 109 RBIs, 317 total bases, and .331 batting average. His stats earned him an All-Star nod and a Silver Slugger Award, but he only placed third in league MVP balloting. Who is this slugger?
   a) Larry Walker
   b) Vladimir Guerrero
   c) Al Oliver
   d) Andres Galarraga

Q82: This veteran won the second batting title in Montreal Expos history. He had 194 hits and led the league in average (.334) and on-base percentage (.413). His stats earned him a sixth consecutive All-Star nod and his first career Silver Slugger Award. Who is this slugger?
   a) Tim Raines
   b) Tim Wallach
   c) Andre Dawson
   d) Andres Galarraga

Q83: Only three players in major-league history had a season like this: 200 hits, 100 runs, 100 RBIs, 35 doubles, 35 home runs, and 40 stolen bases. Alex Rodriguez did it for the Mariners. Alfonso Soriano did it for the Yankees. Who did it for the Nationals/Expos?
   a) Vladimir Guerrero
   b) Bryce Harper
   c) Larry Walker
   d) Andre Dawson

Q84: Any player would love to hit an Opening Day bomb. A home run is great anytime, obviously, but to get the first of the season under your belt so quickly is also a huge confidence boost. Through 2019, who holds the franchise record with home runs in five different Opening Day games?

a) Ryan Zimmerman

b) Gary Carter

c) Ellis Valentine

d) Bryce Harper

Q85: Montreal played its home games at Parc Jarry from 1969-76. The club's record in that time was 285 wins against 356 losses and its leading home run hitter was Bob Bailey with 118 big flies. Who hit a franchise record 58 home runs at Parc Jarry?

a) Bob Bailey

b) Ron Fairly

c) Rusty Staub

d) Mike Jorgensen

Q86: Montreal played all but 43 of its home games at Olympic Stadium from 1977-2004. The remaining games were played at Hiram Bithorn Stadium in San Juan, Puerto Rico, in 2003-04. Which slugger hit a franchise record 126 home runs at Olympic Stadium?

a) Gary Carter

b) Tim Wallach

c) Andre Dawson

d) Vladimir Guerrero

Q87: As long as you get the W, it doesn't matter how you do it. That being said ... there aren't many things in sports better than a walk-off home run. Through 2019, who is the only player in franchise history with 11 walk-off blasts?

   a) Bryce Harper

   b) Vladimir Guerrero

   c) Andre Dawson

   d) Ryan Zimmerman

Q88: The franchise record for consecutive games reaching base by a hit or a walk is 46. It's been done twice. The first player to achieve this feat had an extraordinary .520 on-base percentage with 53 hits and 46 walks. And just for fun he hit a few bombs and slugged .635. Who was the first player in franchise history to reach base safely in 46 consecutive games?

   a) Tim Raines

   b) Andre Dawson

   c) Rusty Staub

   d) Warren Cromartie

Q89: And a follow-up … the first player in franchise history to reach base safely in 46 consecutive games did it over two seasons. The second player did it for the Washington Nationals in a single-season. Who achieved this extraordinary feat?

   a) Jayson Werth

   b) Ryan Zimmerman

   c) Bryce Harper

   d) Ian Desmond

Q90: The Washington Nationals hit just 117 home runs in 2008. Only Minnesota and San Francisco—out of 30 MLB teams—hit fewer on the season. That was the inaugural season for Nationals Park, and the power outage was even worse at home: just 51 bombs on the season. Only Kansas City and San Francisco had fewer bombs at home. Lastings Milledge and Ryan Zimmerman led the club with

14 home runs—and Milledge, Zimmerman, Elijah Dukes, and Ronnie Belliard hit a team-best seven home runs at Nationals Park. Things have obviously improved in recent years. Which slugger hit a record 23 home runs in a single-season at Nationals Park?

a) Adam Dunn

b) Ryan Zimmerman

c) Adam LaRoche

d) Bryce Harper

TOP OF THE FIFTH ANSWER KEY

81: c. Al Oliver (1982).

82: a. Tim Raines (1986).

83: a. Vladimir Guerrero (2002).

84: b. Gary Carter.

85: b. Ron Fairly.

86: d. Vladimir Guerrero.

87: d. Ryan Zimmerman.

88: c. Rusty Staub (1969-70).

89: a. Jayson Werth (2016).

90: d. Bryce Harper (2015).

BOTTOM OF THE FIFTH

Q91: Through 2019, there have been 16 different players with at least one 100-RBI season for the Nationals/Expos. Who had a franchise record *five* such seasons?
a) Vladimir Guerrero
b) Ryan Zimmerman
c) Adam Dunn
d) Tim Wallach

Q92: This slugger's first career grand slam was also his 100th career bomb … who is he?
a) Adam Dunn
b) Ryan Zimmerman
c) Bryce Harper
d) Adam LaRoche

Q93: A hot bat in early April can energize a clubhouse and build a lot of optimism for fans. In franchise history, one player began a season with a 16-game hitting streak. His stats: 23 for 60, with six doubles, two home runs, seven RBIs, and 12 runs. Through 2019, it's the longest hitting streak to begin a season in franchise history. Who began a season in such fine form?
a) Howie Kendrick
b) Willie Davis
c) Tony Tarasco
d) Rusty Staub

Q94: Another impressive streak: this player hit safely in 24 consecutive interleague games (36 for 96, with four doubles, six home runs, 13 RBIs, and 21 runs). Who relentlessly punished the American

League for 24 games over three different seasons?

    a) Jose Vidro

    b) Anthony Rendon

    c) Vladimir Guerrero

    d) Adam LaRoche

Q95: Through 2019, nine players in franchise history had a game with three home runs: Adam Dunn, Ryan Zimmerman, Bryce Harper, Anthony Rendon, Alfonso Soriano, Tim Wallach, Andre Dawson, Larry Parrish, and Gary Carter. Who was the first player to have a three-homer game?

    a) Tim Wallach

    b) Andre Dawson

    c) Larry Parrish

    d) Gary Carter

Q96: Who is the only player in franchise history to hit three home runs in a game … *three times*?

    a) Tim Wallach

    b) Andre Dawson

    c) Larry Parrish

    d) Gary Carter

Q97: Warren Cromartie hit 46 doubles for the Montreal Expos in 1979 to set a franchise record for lefties. That number was later matched by a lefty for the Washington Nationals. Which lefty slugger tied this mark?

    a) Brad Wilkerson

    b) Nick Johnson

    c) Denard Span

    d) Adam LaRoche

Q98: Through 2019, no member of the Washington Nationals has posted a 200-hit season—and only four players ever had a 200-hit season for the Expos: Jose Vidro, Al Oliver, Vladimir Guerrero, and Mark Grudzielanek. Which one achieved that extraordinary feat for the Expos *twice*?

a) Jose Vidro

b) Al Oliver

c) Vladimir Guerrero

d) Mark Grudzielanek

Q99: Through 2019, only one switch-hitter in franchise history has reached base safely by hit or walk in 40 consecutive games. Who achieved this extraordinary feat?

a) Tim Raines

b) Jose Vidro

c) Danny Espinosa

d) Ken Singleton

Q100: Tim Raines had more plate appearances (6,256) than any switch-hitter in franchise history. He was just 22 years old when he led the league with 731 PA in 1982. That number established a franchise record that stood until Trea Turner had 740 PA in 2018. But in 1982, Raines had yet to find his power stroke. He had just four home runs on the season. He went deep 11 times in 1983, while again leading the league with 720 PA—and Raines would eventually hit a career best 18 home runs in 1987. All those plate appearances … but does he hold the career record for most home runs by a switch-hitter? Which switch-hitter belted a franchise record 115 long balls?

a) Tim Raines

b) Jose Vidro

c) Danny Espinosa
d) Ken Singleton

BOTTOM OF THE FIFTH ANSWER KEY

91: a. Vladimir Guerrero.

92: c. Bryce Harper.

93: d. Rusty Staub (1971).

94: c. Vladimir Guerrero (2001-03).

95: d. Gary Carter (1977).

96: c. Larry Parrish (1977, 1978, 1980).

97: b. Nick Johnson (2006).

98: c. Vladimir Guerrero (1998, 2002).

99: a. Tim Raines (1985-86).

100: b. Jose Vidro (1997-2006).

"When you start talking about winning it three times, I can't even comprehend it. It's such an unbelievable feeling and unbelievable moment, you really won't process it until years later."

— *Max Scherzer, after winning his third Cy Young Award*

6 THE HURLERS

In the sixth, it's all about the hurlers. Guys who can paint the corners and throw gas.

Cy Young winners?

Check.

No-hitters?

Check.

Perfection?

Check.

Immaculate innings?

Check.

League leaders, franchise records, mind-blowing stats ... let's get started.

TOP OF THE SIXTH

Q101: This pitcher was the first in franchise history to lead the league in ERA. In 35 starts, he was 19-8 with a 2.40 ERA. In that same season he made his fourth All-Star team and placed second in Cy Young balloting. Who is this pitcher?

    a) Javier Vazquez

    b) Dennis Martinez

    c) Bill Gullickson

    d) Steve Rogers

Q102: An immaculate inning is when you strikeout the side on nine pitches. Who was the first-ever pitcher with an immaculate inning for the Nationals/Expos?

    a) Pedro Martinez

    b) Randy Johnson

    c) Jordan Zimmermann

    d) Max Scherzer

Q103: And a follow-up … who was the first pitcher with *two* immaculate innings for the Nationals/Expos?

    a) Pedro Martinez

    b) Randy Johnson

    c) Jordan Zimmermann

    d) Max Scherzer

Q104: This pitcher no-hit the Dodgers for nine innings on July 26, 1991. The problem was the Expos managed just two hits and couldn't score a run. He lost his no-hitter, shutout, and the game in the tenth inning. Who is this hard-luck pitcher?

    a) Oil Can Boyd

b) Dennis Martinez

c) Brian Barnes

d) Mark Gardner

Q105: And a follow-up ... just two nights later this pitcher took the mound against the Dodgers and tossed the first perfect game and final no-hitter in Montreal Expos history. Who turned in this historic performance?

a) Oil Can Boyd

b) Dennis Martinez

c) Brian Barnes

d) Mark Gardner

Q106: How about the first-ever no-hitter in Expos history? It occurred on April 17, 1969 ... and the guy who threw it? He pitched another one three years later. He's the only player in Expos history with two no-nos. Who achieved this historic feat?

a) Jerry Robertson

b) Bill Stoneman

c) Mike Wegener

d) Steve Renko

Q107: The first no-hitter in Nationals history was on September 28, 2014—the final game of the regular season—vs. the Miami Marlins. This pitcher had 10 strikeouts and would have been perfect if not for a two-out fifth-inning walk to Justin Bour. Who pitched this gem of a game?

a) Gio Gonzalez

b) Doug Fister

c) Tanner Roark

d) Jordan Zimmermann

Q108: Max Scherzer joined the Nationals in 2015 and made an immediate impact. He led the league in complete games and shutouts, was fifth in Cy Young Balloting, and … he became the first pitcher in franchise history with two no-hitters *in one season*. Which teams did Scherzer no-hit in 2015?

    a) Pittsburgh Pirates/New York Mets

    b) Atlanta Braves/Miami Marlins

    c) Philadelphia Phillies/Tampa Bay Rays

    d) San Diego Padres/Colorado Rockies

Q109: This pitcher was the first in franchise history to record double-digit strikeouts in his major-league debut. Who achieved this extraordinary feat?

    a) Reynaldo Lopez

    b) Claudio Vargas

    c) Stephen Strasburg

    d) Brian Barnes

Q110: From 1969-2019, a total of 24 pitchers made Opening Day starts for the Nationals/Expos. Which starter got the nod on Opening Day more than any other pitcher in franchise history?

    a) Livan Hernandez

    b) Dennis Martinez

    c) Steve Rogers

    d) Stephen Strasburg

TOP OF THE SIXTH ANSWER KEY

101: d. Steve Rogers (1982).

102: c. Jordan Zimmermann (May 6, 2011, vs. the Marlins).

103: d. Max Scherzer (May 14, 2017, vs. the Phillies; June 5, 2018, vs. the Blue Jays).

104: d. Mark Gardner.

105: b. Dennis Martinez.

106: b. Bill Stoneman.

107: d. Jordan Zimmermann.

108: a. Pittsburgh Pirates/New York Mets.

109: c. Stephen Strasburg (14 Ks, 2010).

110: c. Steve Rogers (nine).

BOTTOM OF THE SIXTH

Q111: It's a big deal when a pitcher notches 10 strikeouts in one game. To do it in multiple games over the course of a season is even more impressive. And then this guy ... he had a franchise record 18 such games in one season. Who achieved this remarkable feat?

a) Max Scherzer

b) Pedro Martinez

c) Javier Vazquez

d) Stephen Strasburg

Q112: The Montreal Expos record for strikeouts in a single-game is 18. An exact pitch count for his performance isn't available ... but if it were, it's safe to say it wouldn't conform to today's standard. Who struck out 18 Cubs in a complete-game four-hitter?

a) Bill Gullickson

b) Floyd Youmans

c) Mike Wegener

d) Pedro Martinez

Q113: In a two-month stretch, this reliever logged 31 2/3 innings while posting a 1.71 ERA—and he set a Washington Nationals record with 30 consecutive appearances without issuing a single walk. Which hurler set this franchise record?

a) Drew Storen

b) Xavier Cedeno

c) Sean Doolittle

d) Luis Ayala

Q114: In franchise history, one pitcher had a streak of 13 consecutive starts in which he pitched at least seven innings. In a three-month stretch, he logged 102 innings and was 7-3 with a 1.85 ERA. Which hurler set this franchise record?

a) Livan Hernandez

b) Carl Morton

c) Dennis Martinez

d) Steve Rogers

Q115: This pitcher made five consecutive starts in which he totaled 38 2/3 innings with 37 strikeouts … and *zero* walks. That's the best such streak in Nationals history. Who does it belong to?

a) Chien-Ming Wang

b) Jordan Zimmermann

c) Max Scherzer

d) Gio Gonzalez

Q116: In today's game, so much is done to protect arms that complete games are exceedingly rare. In fact, Jordan Zimmermann (2013) and Max Scherzer (2015) are the only Nationals pitchers with as many as four complete games in a season—but that wasn't always the case. Who was the most "recent" pitcher in franchise history with at least 10 complete games in a single-season?

a) Mark Langston

b) Pedro Martinez

c) Dennis Martinez

d) Steve Rogers

Q117: It used to be that when a guy toed the rubber he expected to go nine, whether he had the good stuff or not. Floyd Youmans once tossed a complete game in which he gave up eight earned runs. Steve Rogers is the franchise career leader with 129 complete games—but he was the *losing* pitcher in 27 of those contests. And then this guy: he's the only pitcher in franchise history to give up five earned runs, go the distance, and still get the W ... *twice*. Who achieved this remarkable feat?

a) Steve Renko

b) Ross Grimsley

c) Bill Stoneman

d) Dennis Martinez

Q118: This pitcher was the first in baseball since 1943 to toss a complete game, give up 10 hits and five walks, and lose 1-0. Who was on the mound for this unusual stat line?

a) Livan Hernandez

b) Dennis Martinez

c) Chien-Ming Wang

d) Gio Gonzalez

Q119: Who was the first pitcher in franchise history to record his 1,000th career strikeout while toeing the rubber for the Washington Nationals?

a) Chien-Ming Wang

b) Jordan Zimmermann

c) Max Scherzer

d) Gio Gonzalez

Q120: In 2014, Stephen Strasburg became just the second pitcher in Washington Nationals history to strikeout 200 batters in a single-season. Who was the first pitcher to record a 200-K season for the Nats?

a) Chien-Ming Wang

b) Jordan Zimmermann

c) Livan Hernandez

d) Gio Gonzalez

BOTTOM OF THE SIXTH ANSWER KEY

111: b. Pedro Martinez (1997).

112: a. Bill Gullickson (1980).

113: d. Luis Ayala (2005).

114: c. Dennis Martinez (1992).

115: c. Max Scherzer (2015).

116: b. Pedro Martinez (1997).

117: a. Steve Renko (1970, 1974).

118: a. Livan Hernandez (2004).

119: d. Gio Gonzalez (2014).

120: d. Gio Gonzalez (2012).

"Do my routine, and no change. If it works, I got to keep it going until I retire."

— *Juan Soto*

7 FANTASTIC FEATS

Juan Soto—or, "Childish Bambino"—became the first teenager to hit a major-league home run since, well ... Bryce Harper. It's always a good sign for your organization when the best feats in baseball belong to your team's most popular players.

The seventh is about fantastic feats.

Natural cycles, monster games, exclusive clubs, ridiculous streaks ... and impressive debuts. All that, and more.

Let's get started.

TOP OF THE SEVENTH

Q121: Juan Soto made his big-league debut in May 2018. The 19-year-old outfielder from the Dominican Republic made a big splash—in his first start and second career at-bat, he hit an opposite field three-run home run. The last teenager to hit a big-league home run was Bryce Harper. In fact, Harper holds the NL record for most home runs as a teenager. How many bombs did Harper hit in 2012 when he was 19 years old?

    a) 20

    b) 21

    c) 22

    d) 23

Q122: In baseball history, fewer than 20 players have hit a natural cycle—meaning a single, double, triple, and home run in that exact order. It turns out, the first cycle in franchise history was a natural cycle. Who achieved this fantastic feat?

    a) Chris Speier

    b) Tim Raines

    c) Vladimir Guerrero

    d) Tim Foli

Q123: One player hit for the cycle twice—once for the Expos, and once for the Nationals. Cool, right? Who achieved this extraordinary feat?

    a) Brad Wilkerson

    b) Jose Vidro

    c) Orlando Cabrera

    d) Tony Batista

Q124: The franchise record for hits in a single-game is six. It's been done twice through 2019—and both times included an extraordinary feat aside from the number of hits. Who is the only player in franchise history to hit for the cycle *and* collect six hits in the same game?

    a) Bryce Harper

    b) Larry Walker

    c) Rondell White

    d) Anthony Rendon

Q125: And a follow-up ... who is the only player in major-league history to hit three home runs *and* collect six hits in the same game?

    a) Bryce Harper

    b) Larry Walker

    c) Rondell White

    d) Anthony Rendon

Q126: Coco Laboy played third base in the Expos inaugural game vs. the New York Mets on April 8, 1969. It was also the first game of Laboy's career ... and in the eighth inning, he hit a three-run home run that proved to be the game-winner. Thus, Laboy was the first player in franchise history to homer in his big-league debut. It would take more than a decade before anyone else replicated this feat. Who was the second player in franchise history to go yard in his big-league debut?

    a) Brad Mills

    b) Tim Raines

    c) Tim Wallach

    d) Tony Bernazard

Q127: Through 2019, only one player in franchise history has homered on the very first pitch of his career ... and he was a *pitcher*.

Who hit a three-run home run on the first pitch of his first major-league at-bat?

   a) Ian Krol

   b) Ryan Mattheus

   c) Taylor Jordan

   d) Tommy Milone

Q128: Only four players in major-league history had a 40/40 season—40 home runs, 40 stolen bases. Alex Rodriguez (Seattle, 1998), Barry Bonds (San Francisco, 1996), and Jose Canseco (Oakland, 1988) are all in the club. Which Nationals/Expos player is the fourth member of this exclusive club?

   a) Vladimir Guerrero

   b) Bryce Harper

   c) Larry Walker

   d) Alfonso Soriano

Q129: And a follow-up ... a fifth player nearly had a 40/40 season. He hit a ball that landed on top of the wall and bounced back into play in the second-to-last game of the season. He finished the year with 39 home runs and 40 stolen bases. Which Nationals/Expos player nearly became the fifth member of this exclusive club?

   a) Vladimir Guerrero

   b) Bryce Harper

   c) Larry Walker

   d) Alfonso Soriano

Q130: And one more follow-up ... through 2019, fewer than 50 players in major-league history had a season with 30 home runs and 30 stolen bases. Who is the only player in franchise history with *two* 30/30 seasons?

   a) Vladimir Guerrero

b) Bryce Harper
c) Larry Walker
d) Alfonso Soriano

TOP OF THE SEVENTH ANSWER KEY

121: c. 22.

122: d. Tim Foli (1976).

123: a. Brad Wilkerson (2003, 2005).

124: c. Rondell White (1995).

125: d. Anthony Rendon (2017).

126: c. Tim Wallach (1980).

127: d. Tommy Milone (2011).

128: d. Alfonso Soriano (2006).

129: a. Vladimir Guerrero (2002).

130: a. Vladimir Guerrero (2001, 2002).

BOTTOM OF THE SEVENTH

Q131: Fewer than 10 pitchers in baseball's modern era (since 1903) have pitched at least 150 innings in a season while maintaining a strikeout-to-walk ratio above eight. One did it for the Nationals/Expos. His 8.12 strikeouts-to-walk ratio set a franchise record and remains one of the top-ten ratios in baseball history. Who achieved this extraordinary stat?

    a) Max Scherzer

    b) Pedro Martinez

    c) Javier Vazquez

    d) Stephen Strasburg

Q132: Eight players in franchise history scored at least one run in 10 consecutive games. Through 2019, who is the most recent player to achieve this feat?

    a) Trea Turner

    b) Denard Span

    c) Bryce Harper

    d) Josh Willingham

Q133: This pitcher tossed an Opening Day shutout. And then he did it again one year later. Who achieved this extraordinary feat?

    a) Steve Rogers

    b) Livan Hernandez

    c) Dennis Martinez

    d) Javier Vazquez

Q134: This player was just the fourth in major-league history—alongside Larry Doby, Joe Morgan, and Rickey Henderson—to score four runs in a game without recording an official at-bat. Who did this for the Nationals/Expos?

a) Vladimir Guerrero

b) Bryce Harper

c) Brad Wilkerson

d) Jayson Werth

Q135: It's a special performance when a pitcher tosses a complete-game one-hit shutout ... but what do you get when your starting pitcher also belts a two-run homer in the same game? A once-in-franchise history moment, of course. Who did this for the Montreal Expos?

a) Steve Rogers

b) Floyd Youmans

c) Dennis Martinez

d) Bill Gullickson

Q136: Livan Hernandez (2010) and Gio Gonzalez (2013) both homered during games in which they combined with the Nats' bullpen to pitch a shutout. Through 2019, only one pitcher has homered *and* thrown a complete-game shutout for the Washington Nationals in the same game. Who achieved this remarkable feat?

a) Jordan Zimmermann

b) Max Scherzer

c) Tanner Roark

d) Stephen Strasburg

Q137: This pitcher tossed a complete-game one-hit shutout in his second big-league start. His encore? Another complete-game shutout in his third career start ... and yet another in his ninth career game. Who began his career in such fine form?

a) Scott Sanderson

b) Brian Holman

c) Chris Nabholz

d) Steve Rogers

Q138: Jordan Zimmermann had a streak in 2012 during which he reached base safely in six consecutive starts (he was 7 for 15 with a home run)—tying a Nationals record for pitchers. Max Scherzer also tied this record ... twice: in 2015 (6 for 15) and again in 2018 (6 for 12). The franchise record for pitchers reaching base safely is seven consecutive games. Who achieved this feat (9 for 21, five RBIs, three runs scored) for the Expos?

a) Javier Vazquez

b) Bryn Smith

c) Neal Heaton

d) Bill Gullickson

Q139: In April 1986, Andre Dawson became the first player in franchise history with five or more total bases in four consecutive games. His stats: 9 for 22, with four home runs (all solo). Through 2019, no Nationals/Expos player has ever surpassed that streak. However, one player equaled it ... *twice*. Here are the gaudy numbers: 9 for 16, three doubles, four home runs, eight RBIs, and four runs; then, 10 for 15, six home runs, 14 RBIs, and eight runs. Who had at least five total bases in four consecutive games ... twice?

a) Ryan Zimmerman

b) Bryce Harper

c) Alfonso Soriano

d) Vladimir Guerrero

Q140: Through 2019, eight different shortstops in franchise history had a game with at least five RBIs: Ian Desmond, Jose Macias, Hubie Brooks, Cristian Guzman, Chris Speier, Trea Turner, Danny Espinosa, and Orlando Cabrera. From that list ... which shortstop had *four* such games?

    a) Orlando Cabrera

    b) Hubie Brooks

    c) Chris Speier

    d) Danny Espinosa

BOTTOM OF THE SEVENTH ANSWER KEY

131: a. Max Scherzer (2015).

132: a. Trea Turner (2017).

133: a. Steve Rogers (1982, 1983).

134: b. Bryce Harper (2015).

135: b. Floyd Youmans (August 6, 1986).

136: d. Stephen Strasburg (August 30, 2017).

137: d. Steve Rogers (1973).

138: c. Neal Heaton (1987).

139: d. Vladimir Guerrero (1998, 1999-2000).

140: a. Orlando Cabrera (2000, 2001, 2003).

"This guy carried us throughout the whole season … every team we played circled his name and said 'This guy's not going to beat us,' and with that said, he beat a lot of teams."

— *Mike Rizzo, after Bryce Harper won the 2015 MVP Award*

8 AWARD WINNERS

Whitey Herzog famously said, "We need just two players to be a contender: Babe Ruth and Sandy Koufax."

It's a funny line.

It also underscores a significant truth: baseball is a team game. Even Herzog, in his jest, said *contender*. If you want to be a champion, then you need a team. You don't build a franchise as successful as the Nationals unless the franchise culture embraces that simple fact.

But, the hardware *is* nice.

In the eighth, the trivia is all about award-winning Nationals.

TOP OF THE EIGHTH

Q141: This catcher won three Gold Glove Awards for the Nationals/Expos. He also set a major-league record for fewest passed balls in a season, though ironically it wasn't in one of his Gold Glove campaigns. Who is this award-winning catcher?
 a) Gary Carter
 b) Brian Schneider
 c) Mike Fitzgerald
 d) Michael Barrett

Q142: Two players in Montreal Expos history have won All-Star Game MVP honors. One of them did it twice. Who is this award-winning All-Star?
 a) Tim Raines
 b) Andre Dawson
 c) Gary Carter
 d) Larry Walker

Q143: The other player to win All-Star Game MVP honors for the Montreal Expos was 3-for-3 with a game-winning two-run triple in extra-innings. Who is this award-winning All-Star?
 a) Tim Raines
 b) Andre Dawson
 c) Gary Carter
 d) Larry Walker

Q144: Which two players won both a Gold Glove Award and a Silver Slugger Award in the same season?
 a) Bryce Harper/Jayson Werth
 b) Ian Desmond/Daniel Murphy

c) Ryan Zimmerman/Adam LaRoche

d) Wilson Ramos/Brad Wilkerson

Q145: Max Scherzer became the first pitcher in Nationals history to win the Cy Young Award (and just the sixth pitcher in baseball history to win Cy Young Awards in both the AL and NL). In which categories did Scherzer post league-leading stats during his historic 2016 campaign?

a) Wins, innings, and strikeouts

b) Wins, innings, and ERA

c) Wins, strikeouts, and shutouts

d) Wins, shutouts, and WHIP

Q146: Max Scherzer won a second consecutive Cy Young Award in 2017, and for the first time in franchise history the Nationals had two pitchers place among the top three in balloting. Who was third in Cy Young balloting in 2017?

a) Gio Gonzalez

b) Tanner Roark

c) Stephen Strasburg

d) Sean Doolittle

Q147: The first National League Player of the Month Award was given in 1958. Willie Mays and Stan Musial were co-recipients as both Hall of Fame legends posted insane offensive numbers in May of that year. The Nationals/Expos franchise began play in 1969, but it wasn't until September 1980 that Montreal could boast a Player of the Month Award. Who was the first player in franchise history to receive this honor?

a) Andre Dawson

b) Larry Parrish

c) Rodney Scott

d) Gary Carter

Q148: This slugger won Player of the Month honors a franchise record five times. Who achieved this extraordinary feat?
a) Bryce Harper
b) Vladimir Guerrero
c) Ryan Zimmerman
d) Andre Dawson

Q149: The first Player of the Month recipient in Washington Nationals history took home the award after posting a .367/.450/.622, 7 HR, 22 RBIs slash in 27 games during the month of July. In July of the following season, he took home his second Player of the Month Award when he slashed .337/.446/.687, 6 HR, 24 RBIs in 24 games. Who was the first Player of the Month recipient in Nationals history?
a) Bryce Harper
b) Jayson Werth
c) Ryan Zimmerman
d) Adam Dunn

Q150: The Nationals took home an unprecedented three Player of the Month Awards during the 2016 season—and incredibly, the club began 2017 by winning yet another award for the season's first month. That's a run of four awards in just seven opportunities. Who became the first player in Nationals history to win two Player of the Month Awards in the same season?
a) Daniel Murphy
b) Bryce Harper
c) Anthony Rendon
d) Ryan Zimmerman

TOP OF THE EIGHTH ANSWER KEY

141: a. Gary Carter.

142: c. Gary Carter (1981, 1984).

143: a. Tim Raines (1987).

144: c. Ryan Zimmerman (2009)/Adam LaRoche (2012).

145: a. Wins (20), innings (228 1/3), and strikeouts (284).

146: c. Stephen Strasburg.

147: d. Gary Carter (32 G, .320/.403/.648, 13 HR, 36 RBIs).

148: b. Vladimir Guerrero (July 1998, August 1999, April 2000, April 2002, August 2003).

149: b. Jayson Werth (July 2013, July 2014).

150: a. Daniel Murphy (May and July 2016).

BOTTOM OF THE EIGHTH

Q151: The National League Pitcher of the Month Award was first given in 1975. It was April 1978 when a member of the Expos' staff won the award for the first time. Who was the first recipient of the Pitcher of the Month Award?

a) Steve Rogers

b) Ross Grimsley

c) Rudy May

d) Dan Schatzeder

Q152: The first recipient of Pitcher of the Month honors for the Washington Nationals did so during the inaugural 2005 season. Who was the best pitcher in the NL during June 2005?

a) Livan Hernandez

b) Esteban Loaiza

c) John Patterson

d) Chad Cordero

Q153: Through 2019, Max Scherzer has won a franchise best six National League Pitcher of the Month Awards. How many times did he win the award in consecutive months?

a) 0

b) 1

c) 2

d) 3

Q154: The National League Rookie of the Month Award was first given in 2001. Albert Pujols won the inaugural award in April for the St. Louis Cardinals, and then he won it again in May. Who was the first player in Nationals history to win Rookie of the Month honors?

a) Endy Chavez

b) Terrmel Sledge

c) Ryan Zimmerman

d) Brad Wilkerson

Q155: A handful of Nationals players won Rookie of the Month honors multiple times. Who was the first to win the award three times?

a) Stephen Strasburg

b) Bryce Harper

c) Trea Turner

d) Juan Soto

Q156: Bryce Harper was the first player in franchise history to win league MVP honors. Harper, who was 22 years old, was the youngest unanimous MVP in baseball history—and he gave credit to a teammate for helping him with his mental approach. Harper said: "[He's] such a great teammate. He is a great person on and off the field. I enjoy being around him … At the end of the day, if you are 0-for-4 or 4-for-4, you have to have the same mentality coming in the next day. That's what I tried to do the whole year." Who did Harper credit for helping him with this approach?

a) Ryan Zimmerman

b) Jayson Werth

c) Denard Span

d) Ian Desmond

Q157: In the seven seasons preceding Bryce Harper's big league debut, the Nationals scored 4,688 runs—an average of 4.134 per game. In seven seasons with Harper (2012-18), the Nationals scored 5,129 runs—an average of 4.517 per game. Bryce Harper won Rookie of the Year and MVP honors, and he was a six-time All-Star.

He hit 184 home runs with 521 RBIs and 610 runs scored. And yet ... how many Silver Slugger Awards did Harper win?

a) 0

b) 1

c) 2

d) 3

Q158: Bryce Harper won the Best Baseball Player ESPY Award in 2016, after his monstrous 2015 MVP campaign. It was the first ESPY win for a Nationals player. In a Q&A with ESPN during ESPY week, which baseball legend did Harper reveal as his very "first big league baseball hero"?

a) Frank Thomas

b) Craig Biggio

c) Derek Jeter

d) Roberto Alomar

Q159: The Nationals selected Anthony Rendon as the overall #6 pick in the first-round of the 2011 draft. For which university did Rendon win the *Baseball America* College Player of the Year Award in 2010?

a) UCLA

b) Rice

c) Houston

d) Florida State

Q160: Who was the first manager in Washington Nationals history to win the prestigious Manager of the Year Award?

a) Davey Johnson

b) Manny Acta

c) Matt Williams

d) Dusty Baker

BOTTOM OF THE EIGHTH ANSWER KEY

151: b. Ross Grimsley (4 G, 4-0, 1.53, 11 Ks).

152: d. Chad Cordero (16 G, 12 SV, 0.82, 13 Ks).

153: c. 2 (May and June 2015, April and May 2018).

154: a. Endy Chavez (September 2002).

155: d. Juan Soto (June, July, and September 2018).

156: d. Ian Desmond.

157: b. 1.

158: c. Derek Jeter.

159: b. Rice.

160: a. Davey Johnson (2012).

"Stuff doesn't bother us … You've just got to do it. You've got to show up tomorrow ready to eat somebody's face."

— *Jayson Werth*

9 THE TEAMS

As we move to the ninth, we take a look at some of the greatest moments in team history. Timely hitting? Absolutely. Dominant pitching? Some of the best in the game.

Franchise records?

Ridiculously long streaks?

Division titles?

Check, *check*, and *check*. Let's get started.

TOP OF THE NINTH

Q161: Max Scherzer tied a major-league record with 20 strikeouts on May 11, 2016. Incredibly, 96 of his 119 pitches were strikes and he didn't walk a single batter—though he did induce 33 swings and misses, which was the second highest total in the major-leagues over the previous 15 years. He caught six guys looking—the rest went down swinging. Against which team was Scherzer so dominant?

a) New York Yankees

b) Boston Red Sox

c) Detroit Tigers

d) Chicago White Sox

Q162: A month later, Scherzer struck out nine of the first 10 batters he faced in a match-up against the team with the best record in baseball. He took a perfect game into the sixth inning and finished with a 4-1 victory. Against which MLB-best team was Scherzer so dominant?

a) Chicago Cubs

b) Cleveland Indians

c) Los Angeles Dodgers

d) San Francisco Giants

Q163: The Nationals were dead last or second-to-last for six consecutive seasons to begin their tenure in D.C., but a string of solid draft picks began the club's ascent to perennial playoff contender. In which season did Washington finally meet expectations and claim the first NL East title in Nationals history?

a) 2011

b) 2012

c) 2013

d) 2014

Q164: The second NL East title in Nationals history was a romp—
17 games over the second place club. What made it sweeter was the
fact Washington clinched on the road against a division rival. In
which ballpark did the Nationals celebrate a second division crown in
three seasons?
  a) Citi Field
  b) Marlins Park
  c) Turner Field
  d) Citizens Bank Park

Q165: The Expos won a franchise record 13 consecutive home games
in August and September 1979. The longest home winning streak in
Nationals history is 12 games. In which season did the Nationals go
15-2 at home—including 12 straight victories—during the month of
June?
  a) 2005
  b) 2009
  c) 2013
  d) 2017

Q166: Montreal won a franchise best 10 consecutive games on three
occasions: August to September 1979, June 1980, and June 1997.
The Nationals won 10 straight to tie that mark in 2005. Through
2019, only one other Nationals club has posted a 10-game winning
streak—and they did it with a lot of drama. In which season did the
Nationals post a 10-game winning streak that included five walk-off
victories?
  a) 2010
  b) 2012
  c) 2014

d) 2016

Q167: The Montreal Expos set a franchise record in 1996 when its pitching staff—led by Jeff Fassero and Pedro Martinez—recorded 1,206 strikeouts on the season. That record fell in 2012 when the Nationals—led by Gio Gonzalez and Stephen Strasburg—struck out 1,325 batters. In which season did the pitching staff establish yet another record—and reach a remarkable milestone—by striking out 1,511 opposing batters?
   a) 2016
   b) 2017
   c) 2018
   d) 2019

Q168: Through 2019, only once in franchise history have the Nationals won three Pitcher of the Month Awards in a single-season. And to give you an idea how little teams outside the division wanted to play the NL East, the other three awards went to the Braves (2) and Mets (1). In which season did the Nationals dominate NL hitters in such unprecedented fashion?
   a) 2011
   b) 2012
   c) 2013
   d) 2014

Q169: Anthony Rendon's 20th home run of 2016 was also the Nationals 200th of the season—and it was the first time in franchise history that the club reached that milestone. From 2016-19, the Nationals would total three 200-homer seasons. In which season did the offense slug a franchise best 231 long balls?
   a) 2016
   b) 2017

c) 2018

d) 2019

Q170: Montreal beat Atlanta by a sandlot score at Fulton County Stadium on July 30, 1978. The Expos hit a franchise record eight home runs and won the contest 19-0. Through 2019, it remains the largest blowout in franchise history. In recent years, a Nationals club tied the eight homers in a game record—and did so in historic fashion. In a home contest vs. the Brewers, Brian Goodwin, Wilmer Difo, Bryce Harper, and Ryan Zimmerman tied a major-league record by smashing four consecutive home runs. The Nationals became just the eighth team in history to achieve this feat. Two batters after Zimmerman's bomb, Anthony Rendon hit another one—which made the Nats just the sixth team in history with five home runs in a single inning. Harper and Zimmerman each homered twice in the game and Jose Lobaton got in on the action as well for the record-tying total of eight team home runs. In which season did the offense (with Max Scherzer on the mound, no less) punish the Brewers in a historic beat down?

a) 2015

b) 2016

c) 2017

d) 2018

TOP OF THE NINTH ANSWER KEY

161: c. Detroit Tigers.

162: a. Chicago Cubs.

163: b. 2012.

164: c. Turner Field (September 16, 2014).

165: a. 2005.

166: c. 2014 (August 12-21, 2014).

167: d. 2019.

168: b. 2012 (Stephen Strasburg, April; Gio Gonzalez, May; and Jordan Zimmermann, July).

169: d. 2019.

170: c. 2017.

BOTTOM OF THE NINTH

Q171: Silver Slugger Awards are given to the best offensive player at each position, in each league. A lot of big names have won the award in franchise history: Gary Carter, Andre Dawson, Tim Wallach, Tim Raines, and Larry Walker, just to name a few. The first recipient in Nationals history was Alfonso Soriano in 2006. Clubs aren't guaranteed anything when it comes to these awards—which is why it was a pretty big deal when the Nationals later had three recipients of the Silver Slugger Award in the same season. Which club can claim this remarkable achievement?
  a) 2012
  b) 2013
  c) 2014
  d) 2015

Q172: Washington set a franchise record in 2019 when the offense averaged 5.39 runs per game—only the Dodgers (5.47) scored more often—and it was just the second time in Nationals history that the club averaged more than five runs per game. Which Nationals club was the first to average five runs per game for an entire season?
  a) 2015
  b) 2016
  c) 2017
  d) 2018

Q173: The 1979 Montreal Expos set a franchise record with 18 team shutouts. In 13 of those contests the starting pitcher went the distance. In recent years, the Washington Nationals established a new franchise record by pitching 19 team shutouts in a single-season— however, predictably, given the attitude toward pitch counts in today's game, in only four of those contests did the starting pitcher go the distance. Which Nationals club set a franchise record with 19 team shutouts?

a) 2019

b) 2014

c) 2016

d) 2011

Q174: In 2006, the Nationals had 43 games with at least five extra-base hits—but the pitching was so abysmal that the club's record in those games was only 27-16. Fast-forward a few years, and the Nationals had a season in which the offense tallied five or more extra-base hits in an astounding 45 different games. A solid pitching rotation meant that club was 37-8 when the offense flipped the power switch. Which Nationals club had 45 games with at least five extra-base hits?

a) 2016

b) 2017

c) 2018

d) 2019

Q175: The Nationals won division titles in 2012, 2014, 2016, and 2017. In which of those seasons did the pitching staff set franchise records while giving up the fewest earned runs and fewest total runs in the league?

a) 2012

b) 2014

c) 2016

d) 2017

Q176: The 1979 Montreal Expos won 95 games but placed second in the division by two games. That 95 wins represents the highest season total in Expos history. In which season did the Nationals win a division title and set a new franchise record with 98 regular season victories?

    a) 2012
    b) 2014
    c) 2016
    d) 2017

Q177: In 2005, the Nationals were a .500 club at 81-81 during their inaugural season in D.C. But for the six years that followed (2006-11) the club was mired in sub-.500 mediocrity. Four last place finishes. Below .500 every season. But the draft picks that resulted from such poor play led to Stephen Strasburg, Bryce Harper, and Anthony Rendon ... and from 2012-19 the club has five seasons with 93-plus wins, four division titles, a wild card, and no losing records during the regular season. In which season did the Washington Nationals finally win enough games to erase 2006-11 and lift its franchise record above the .500 mark?

    a) 2016
    b) 2017
    c) 2018
    d) 2019

Q178: And a follow-up to that last question ... in which year did *Baseball America* rank the Washington Nationals' minor league system as the best in MLB?

    a) 2009
    b) 2010
    c) 2011
    d) 2012

Q179: The Nationals began play in Washington in 2005 at RFK

Stadium. In which year did the club officially break ground on what would become Nationals Park?

a) 2004

b) 2005

c) 2006

d) 2007

Q180: Five runs is the modern definition of a blowout. The 1987 Expos won 25 such games. Through 2019, six different Nationals teams have surpassed that mark. Better offense? Better pitching? Both, really. In which season did the Nationals win a franchise best 32 games by five or more runs?

a) 2016

b) 2017

c) 2018

d) 2019

BOTTOM OF THE NINTH ANSWER KEY

171: a. 2012 (Ian Desmond, Adam LaRoche, Stephen Strasburg).

172: c. 2017 (5.06).

173: b. 2014.

174: b. 2017.

175: b. 2014 (555 R, 495 ER).

176: a. 2012.

177: d. 2019.

178: d. 2012.

179: c. 2006.

180: b. 2017.

"It's amazing watching him. It can get kind of boring when he's striking everybody out."

— *Anthony Rendon, on the pitching success of teammate Stephen Strasburg*

10 EXTRA INNINGS

There is no clock in baseball. You have to get 27 outs, and then you can go home. That's why you never leave a game early. You just don't know what's going to happen next.

But sometimes 27 outs isn't enough.

It's free baseball, and it could go all night. Tense. Exhilarating. And conventional wisdom is tossed. Everything is on the table, because all it takes to win is a single run.

That's why here in extras we've got a bit of everything trivia-wise: gutsy performances, All-Star game heroics, more franchise records, and even some football.

Finish strong ...

TOP OF THE TENTH

Q181: The first game in franchise history was on the road at Shea Stadium on Tuesday, April 8, 1969. The Expos defeated the Mets, 11-10. Who was the first-ever starting pitcher for the Montreal Expos?

a) Bill Stoneman
b) Jerry Robertson
c) Mike Wegener
d) Mudcat Grant

Q182: Second baseman Gary Sutherland was 0-for-6 in that inaugural game vs. New York ... however, he reached on a first-inning error and later scored. Whose double scored Sutherland to account for the first hit, run, and RBI in franchise history?

a) Maury Wills
b) Rusty Staub
c) Mack Jones
d) Bob Bailey

Q183: The first-ever home run for the Montreal Expos was hit by a pitcher ... and it was the only home run of his career. Which pitcher achieved this historic first against Hall of Fame legend Tom Seaver?

a) Jerry Robertson
b) Don Shaw
c) Dan McGinn
d) Carroll Sembera

Q184: The Expos traded future Hall of Fame catcher Gary Carter to the New York Mets in December 1984. Carter would go on to win the 1986 World Series with the Mets. Meanwhile, the package of players sent to Montreal for Carter included Mike Fitzgerald, Herm Winningham, Floyd Youmans, and ... this player, who paid immediate dividends with back-to-back Silver Slugger Awards and two All-Star selections in his first three seasons in Montreal. Who was the fourth player that came over from the Mets in the Gary Carter trade?

   a) Vance Law

   b) Luis Rivera

   c) Hubie Brooks

   d) Mitch Webster

Q185: In a game vs. Minnesota that he would later describe as both the "Twilight Zone" and "a roller coaster," manager Dusty Baker told one of his players: "If we have an opportunity to pinch-hit you and you can hit a homer, that would be great." Down a run in the ninth, that player hit a pinch-homer to send the game into extra-innings (and the Nats would go on to win 6-5 in 16 innings). From which player did Dusty Baker request (and get) a game-tying home run?"

   a) Ryan Zimmerman

   b) Danny Espinosa

   c) Bryce Harper

   d) Jose Lobaton

Q186: In 2014, Ian Desmond became just the fourth shortstop in major-league history—alongside Alex Rodriguez, Jimmy Rollins, and Hanley Ramirez—with three seasons of 20 home runs and 20 steals. Desmond holds franchise records for shortstops with 913 games, 110 home runs, and 122 stolen bases. However ... does he hold the record for career multi-homer games as a shortstop? Which player holds this franchise record?

   a) Orlando Cabrera

b) Ian Desmond

c) Trea Turner

d) Cristian Guzman

Q187: Jordan Zimmermann's no-hitter vs. Miami in the 2014 season finale was the first no-no in the nation's capital since Bobby Burke for the Washington Senators no-hit the Boston Red Sox on August 8, 1931. Zimmermann's bid at history was nearly derailed by a line drive off the bat of Christian Yelich. Whose remarkable defensive grab preserved the first-ever no-hitter in Washington Nationals history?

a) Michael A. Taylor

b) Ian Desmond

c) Steven Souza Jr.

d) Anthony Rendon

Q188: Cristian Guzman set a Nationals franchise record with 183 hits in 2008. His record would last until the very same season-finale in which Jordan Zimmermann tossed his remarkable no-hitter. Whose third-inning double vs. the Marlins was his 184th hit of the season and a new Nationals record?

a) Ian Desmond

b) Anthony Rendon

c) Bryce Harper

d) Denard Span

Q189: A walk-off home run gave the Nationals a 5-2 victory over the Braves on September 4, 2015. It was the very first pinch-hit home run in Washington Nationals history, and it was also the first walk-off home run and first pinch-hit home run in the career of the guy who sent the crowd home happy. Whose heroics made history that day?

a) Trea Turner

b) Michael A. Taylor

c) Wilmer Difo

d) Anthony Rendon

Q190: In Max Scherzer's no-hitter vs. Pittsburgh on June 20, 2015, he was perfect through 8 2/3 innings. In his second no-no of the season vs. the New York Mets on October 3, Scherzer set franchise records with nine consecutive strikeouts from the sixth to ninth inning and 17 total for the game. In both games, only one runner reached base. How did Scherzer lose his perfect game bids in 2015?

a) Walk/fielding error

b) Walk/walk

c) Walk/hit-by-pitch

d) Hit-by-pitch/fielding error

TOP OF THE TENTH ANSWER KEY

181: d. Mudcat Grant.

182: d. Bob Bailey.

183: c. Dan McGinn.

184: c. Hubie Brooks.

185: c. Bryce Harper.

186: c. Trea Turner (3, through 2019; Danny Espinosa also had 3 from 2010-16).

187: c. Steven Souza Jr.

188: d. Denard Span.

189: b. Michael A. Taylor.

190: d. Hit-by-pitch/fielding error.

BOTTOM OF THE TENTH

Q191: The NFL Pepsi PUNT, PASS & KICK competition is the oldest NFL Youth Football program. Its first competition was held in 1961. Which Montreal Expos star was a PP&K National Champion as a kid?

a) Vladimir Guerrero

b) Larry Walker

c) Tim Raines

d) Gary Carter

Q192: This player had a historic four-game series against the Reds. He homered from both sides of the plate in two of those games. He totaled five home runs—including two grand slams—for the series, and he had 15 RBIs. Which player had this extraordinary series?

a) Jose Vidro

b) Tim Raines

c) David Segui

d) Danny Espinosa

Q193: From 1969-2019, the Nationals/Expos won 14 games that featured both a shutout and a walk-off. The score in 13 of those contests was 1-0. The most recent was in August 2014 when Anthony Rendon singled to score Denard Span after Gio Gonzalez teamed with Matt Thornton and Rafael Soriano to blank the Diamondbacks for nine innings. In 1983, however, the Expos had a shutout and a walk-off that stands alone in franchise history. It's happened only the one time ... a walk-off grand slam, with two outs no less. Who is the only player in franchise history to walk-off a shutout victory with a grand slam?

a) Tim Raines

b) Tim Wallach

c) Gary Carter

d) Andre Dawson

Q194: Andre Dawson was the first player in franchise history to hit safely in eight consecutive plate appearances when he did so from June 4-7, 1983. Dmitri Young tied that record from May 31 to June 1, 2007. Who was the third player in franchise history—and the first to do it as a rookie—to hit safely in eight consecutive plate appearances?

a) Juan Soto

b) Bryce Harper

c) Victor Robles

d) Trea Turner

Q195: Nelson Santovenia made history on September 3, 1988, when he became the first rookie in franchise history to hit a walk-off home run for his second long ball of the game. Brian Schneider would match that feat in 2003. Who was the first rookie to hit two home runs in a game—including a walk-off—for the Washington Nationals?

a) Anthony Rendon

b) Ryan Zimmerman

c) Trea Turner

d) Juan Soto

Q196: This player hit for the cycle and drove home seven runs. It was just the eighth time in major-league history that a player had seven-plus RBIs while hitting for the cycle. Who achieved this remarkable feat for the Nationals?

a) Christian Guzman

b) Brad Wilkerson

c) Anthony Rendon

d) Trea Turner

Q197: In 2017, this pitcher set a franchise record by tossing 35 consecutive scoreless innings. Who achieved this remarkable feat?

a) Gio Gonzalez

b) Stephen Strasburg

c) Max Scherzer

d) Tanner Roark

Q198: This player was the first in franchise history to homer in an All-Star Game, the first to have two home runs in the same All-Star Game, and he remains the only player in franchise history with three career All-Star home runs. Who is this all-time great?

a) Andre Dawson

b) Tim Wallach

c) Gary Carter

d) Vladimir Guerrero

Q199: The Nationals won a grueling contest, 8-5, on the road in LA on September 3, 2014. It took 14 innings and was the longest game by time the Nationals had ever played: 5 hours and 34 minutes. The hero for the Nats took the field with back tightness, a bruised elbow, and the flu … and all he did was hit a game-tying home run in the ninth inning, a go-ahead single in the 12th, and a game-winning RBI that he legged out for a fielder's choice in the 14th. Whose gutsy performance gave the Nationals a crucial road victory in the stretch run to a division title in 2014?

a) Ryan Zimmerman

b) Jayson Werth

c) Danny Espinosa

d) Adam LaRoche

Q200: Ryan Zimmerman was the first player to hit 200 career home runs exclusively with the Nationals. No one else is even close to the 270 total Zimmerman hit from 2005-19. How many times did Zimmerman hit 30 home runs in a season?

a) 0

b) 1

c) 2

d) 3

BOTTOM OF THE TENTH ANSWER KEY

191: d. Gary Carter.

192: d. Danny Espinosa.

193: a. Tim Raines.

194: d. Trea Turner (August 23-24, 2016).

195: d. Trea Turner (September 9, 2016).

196: d. Trea Turner (April 25, 2017).

197: b. Stephen Strasburg.

198: c. Gary Carter.

199: d. Adam LaRoche.

200: c. 2 (2009, 2017).

"We started off horrible, as we all know, and we vowed that we wouldn't quit. I told the boys, 'I promise you, stay with it, don't quit, this will turn around.'"

— *Dave Martinez*

11 STAY IN THE FIGHT

The final out of the 2019 World Series was a moment 15 years in the making. It had been building to this ever since the Washington Nationals used the fourth overall pick in the 2005 draft to select Ryan Zimmerman. From the University of Virginia to the majors in the span of a few weeks, young and talented and filled with optimism—Zimmerman had every reason to believe this moment would one day arrive. Only he could never have imagined it in quite this way. Not after years of misfires, missed chances, seasons lost to injury—the distractions, frustrations, and underwhelming teams that were loaded with more talent than any organization could ever possibly deserve. But what is important, and the lesson baseball always seems to teach us, is this: perseverance.

In his own words: "Unbelievable. World champion. No one can ever take it away from me."

Zimmerman and his teammates will get rings.

Juan Soto after two years. Zimmerman after 15. Maybe there

will be more for each of them, or maybe this is it.

Just five months and a couple days before Zimmerman and his teammates hoisted the Commissioner's Trophy, Barry Svrluga wrote a column for the Washington post titled: "*Who cares about Dave Martinez? In a lost season, Nationals face tougher decisions.*"

It's true. Rumors were swirling.

Dave Martinez would be fired. Max Scherzer would be dealt. The Nationals were 12 games under .500, so one could forgive Svrluga for his lack of faith.

He had no idea "Baby Shark" was on its way.

Or "Childish Bambino" was going to make Nationals Park his personal backyard sandlot. Or Mad Max was going to take the mound with a broken face and throw seven scoreless against Bryce Harper and the Phillies. Or Ant would abuse NL pitchers until he'd rewritten half the Nationals' record books. Or Truck would find the Fountain of Youth.

If you really want to know the most asinine headline of the year, it was on ESPN.com after the Nationals clinched a playoff berth. It seems ESPN had "Boldly" predicted in spring training that Washington was going to be really, really good in 2019.

Great job, guys. Pat yourself on the back.

Fifteen NL clubs. Three division champions. Two wild cards. And the Nationals' rotation was anchored by Scherzer and Strasburg.

Really bold.

This Nationals team was always going to make the playoffs. And Ryan Zimmerman was not going to go 0-for-5 in postseason chances.

Stay in the fight.

World Series champions.

And congratulations to you, the diehard fans. This is your moment as well. The Nationals know it. The entire baseball world knows it. Revels are earned. It took 15 years, but revels are earned.

2019 REGULAR SEASON

Q201: The Nationals were six games under .500 when play began on June 14, but that night, home runs by Anthony Rendon and Howie Kendrick powered the club to a 7-3 victory over Arizona and began a franchise record streak. In how many consecutive games did the Nationals hit at least one home run during June and July (while climbing to five games over .500 and back into the postseason picture)?

 a) 19

 b) 20

 c) 21

 d) 22

Q202: Anthony Rendon set career highs in 2017 when he hit 25 home runs and drove in 100 runs—and then he shattered both in 2019, as it took him 35 fewer games to reach 100 RBIs. Dave Martinez would later say: "It's a testament to what he's done all year. He's been really good … and we still have five weeks to play." Rendon would finish the regular season with a franchise record 126 RBIs. Who held the previous record of 110 RBIs?

 a) Bryce Harper

 b) Ryan Zimmerman

 c) Adam Dunn

 d) Adam LaRoche

Q203: Yan Gomes was behind the dish for this pitcher's immaculate inning—just the fourth in Nationals history—against the Miami Marlins on July 3. Gomes would later say about the game itself: "He was moving the ball back and forth unbelievable. And then when he needed to make a pitch, it was right there … he never gave in. He battled his tail off." Who made history against the Marlins that night?

a) Patrick Corbin

b) Max Scherzer

c) Anibal Sanchez

d) Stephen Strasburg

Q204: Stephen Strasburg was 5-0 in July with a 1.44 ERA and 44 strikeouts—and he obviously won NL Pitcher of the Month honors—but that was just the beginning of a sustained run of dominance that continued through October. How many games did the Nationals win during Strasburg's 18 starts from June 21 through the end of the regular season?

a) 11

b) 13

c) 15

d) 17

Q205: Strasburg's historic July came on the heels of Max Scherzer's record setting June. Scherzer—who won NL Pitcher of the Month honors for the sixth time—became the first pitcher in Nationals history to go 6-0 in one calendar month. Pundits might have been quick to write off the 2019 Nationals after their horrendous start to the season—but with Strasburg and Scherzer it's easy to see why Nationals fans never quit believing in this team. How many games did the Nationals win during Scherzer's 15 starts from June 2 through the end of the regular season?

a) 10

b) 11

c) 12

d) 13

Q206: For any young fans reading this book some years in the future, trying to learn your team's history for the first time ... here's everything you need to know about Max Scherzer and the type of competitor he was on the field. As he reeled off that 6-0 record in June, he broke his nose while attempting to bunt in batting practice. And took the mound the next night against former teammate Bryce Harper and the division-rival Phillies. Adrian Garro on MLB.com said it best: "This is next level stuff." You bet it is. Dude's face was broken. Most guys would have been on the IL for weeks. Instead: Seven innings, four hits, 10 Ks—no runs. Nationals momentum continued to build, and after that game, anyone who thought this club might really miss the playoffs wasn't seriously paying attention. The rest of the rotation had no choice but to step up their game as well—and from June through September it reeled off one quality start after another. A staggering 44 quality starts in essentially three months. The Nationals led the league the rest of the season in converting quality starts to wins. What was the Nationals record in those 44 games?

a) 39-5

b) 40-4

c) 41-3

d) 42-2

Q207: A quality start is defined as six innings with no more than three earned runs. All season Jacob deGrom, Clayton Kershaw, and Hyun-Jin Ryu got headlines and accolades—and well-deserved, as they all tallied 22 or more quality starts in a season that redefined what we mean by "juiced." As balls left the park in record numbers, however, it was a member of the Nats' rotation who actually *led the league* in quality starts. Who made an extraordinary 24 quality starts for the Nationals?

a) Stephen Strasburg

b) Patrick Corbin

c) Max Scherzer

d) Anibal Sanchez

Q208: Washington's longest hitting streak of the season was 17 games. In the early season struggles, he was the guy who carried the team until everything finally began to click. In the 17-game streak, he had 26 hits, 10 doubles, six home runs, and 18 RBIs—and he also set a Nationals record with at least one extra-base hit in 10 consecutive games. Who was the Nationals' offensive star in early April?

a) Anthony Rendon

b) Juan Soto

c) Trea Turner

d) Victor Robles

Q209: In the third week of May, the Nationals were swept by the Mets at Citi Field and fell to a season worse 12 games under .500 at 19-31. But by the time Washington hosted New York in early September, the Nationals were on a 9-1 run and a season high 19 games over .500—and in that series the club produced a signature win that put the rest of the league on notice: You don't want to face this club in October. The Mets led game two of that series 10-4 going to the bottom of the ninth, but the Nationals scored seven times for the win. The Mets had never blown a lead that big in their history. The Nationals had never overcome a deficit that big in their history. But it happened. Who hit a three-run home run to walk-off that historic contest vs. the Mets?

a) Matt Adams

b) Howie Kendrick

c) Kurt Suzuki

d) Gerardo Parra

Q210: Washington had seven walk-off victories during the 2019 regular season. Four home runs, one double, one single, and one that was a literal walk-off, as in a bases loaded walk. Five different batters got in on the fun ... but which one led the club with *three* walk-off hits (including two home runs)?

a) Kurt Suzuki

b) Anthony Rendon

c) Matt Adams

d) Trea Turner

2019 REGULAR SEASON ANSWER KEY

201: c. 21 (16-5 record).

202: b. Ryan Zimmerman (2006).

203: d. Stephen Strasburg.

204: b. 13 (Strasburg was 11-2).

205: c. 12 (Scherzer was 9-2).

206: c. 41-3.

207: b. Patrick Corbin.

208: a. Anthony Rendon.

209: c. Kurt Suzuki.

210: d. Trea Turner.

2019 POSTSEASON

Q211: Washington won a season high eight in a row and nine and out of 10 to close out the regular season—and the offense outscored its opponents in that stretch, 54-24. It's easy to see why Milwaukee—minus Christian Yelich—was a severe underdog as the Nationals hosted the Brewers in the Wild Card Game. But it's the playoffs. If you make it, you can win it. And nothing is more of a crapshoot than a one-game playoff ... and sure enough, Milwaukee led 3-1 in the eighth inning. Josh Hader—with 37 saves on the season—was on the mound, and the Nationals were down to their final four outs. Whose pinch-hit single ignited a three-run rally that won the game and saved the season?

a) Andrew Stevenson
b) Michael A. Taylor
c) Brian Dozier
d) Ryan Zimmerman

Q212: Juan Soto won the Wild Card Game with a clutch two-out single that plated three runs—and in the process he became the second youngest player in major-league history to win a postseason game with a hit in the eighth inning or later. Soto's clutch hit was the first of many for the Nationals in the 2019 postseason. Who led the club with four "clutch late and close game" hits throughout the postseason?

a) Anthony Rendon
b) Juan Soto
c) Howie Kendrick
d) Ryan Zimmerman

Q213: In 2017, the Nationals lost their fourth consecutive Division

Series—this time to the Cubs. It was the third time in four trips to the playoffs that the Nationals lost in a decisive Game 5—and all three of those losses came at home. Apparently the Nationals have better luck on the road—at least in the 2019 playoffs. The club overcame long odds to win Game 5 of the NLDS on the road in Los Angeles, 7-3 in 10 innings. In fact, the Nationals won on something that had never happened in major-league history ... who was the first player—*ever*—to hit a grand slam in extra-innings of a postseason game on the road?

    a) Trea Turner

    b) Juan Soto

    c) Howie Kendrick

    d) Victor Robles

Q214: That grand slam was made possible courtesy of back-to-back home runs—on consecutive pitches, no less—against the Dodgers' Clayton Kershaw. Down 3-1 in the top of the eighth, which duo went back-to-back to set the stage for an historic extra-inning victory?

    a) Trea Turner/Adam Eaton

    b) Adam Eaton/Anthony Rendon

    c) Anthony Rendon/Juan Soto

    d) Juan Soto/Ryan Zimmerman

Q215: In the NLCS vs. the Cardinals, this pitcher became just the sixth in major-league history to throw 7 2/3 no-hit innings in a postseason game. He also became the first pitcher *ever* to throw at least six hitless innings in two different postseasons. Who achieved this historic feat as the Nationals swept the Cardinals to claim the first pennant in franchise history?

    a) Anibal Sanchez

    b) Stephen Strasburg

c) Max Scherzer

d) Patrick Corbin

Q216: There were 757 intentional walks across Major League Baseball in 2019. The Houston Astros were the only team—from either league—that did not intentionally walk a single batter the entire season. That is, until Game 2 of the World Series. Whose bat were the Astros so afraid of?

a) Juan Soto

b) Trea Turner

c) Anthony Rendon

d) Howie Kendrick

Q217: Washington was 12-5 in its October run to the World Series title. What was the combined won-loss record of Stephen Strasburg and Max Scherzer?

a) 8-0

b) 7-1

c) 6-2

d) 5-3

Q218: The Astros' Gerrit Cole had an historic regular season campaign, and the Astros had home-field advantage in the World Series with Cole slated to start Game 1—so when the Astros scored two runs in the first, their fans felt pretty good about things. But then this guy answered in the second with the first World Series home run in Nationals history. Whose long ball got the Nats on the board in a game they would go on to win 5-4?

a) Juan Soto

b) Ryan Zimmerman

c) Victor Robles

d) Howie Kendrick

Q219: This player was the offensive star of the World Series. Who led the club in runs, hits, and home runs?

a) Anthony Rendon

b) Howie Kendrick

c) Juan Soto

d) Trea Turner

Q220: Zack Greinke had a one-hit shutout through six innings of Game 7—and with a two-run lead, it seemed like the Astros were in control. But then Anthony Rendon and Howie Kendrick turned Game 7 around with a solo blast and a two-run home run in the seventh inning. After rallying to beat Milwaukee in the Wild Card Game, rallying to beat LA in the Division Series, forcing a Game 7 in the World Series, and then rallying to win Game 7 … this player summed it up best: "This is now the most 2019 Nats thing to ever happen. Another elimination game, another come-from-behind win."

a) Kurt Suzuki

b) Gerardo Parra

c) Dave Martinez

d) Sean Doolittle

2019 POSTSEASON ANSWER KEY

211: d. Ryan Zimmerman.

212: c. Howie Kendrick (4 for 6, two home runs, eight RBIs).

213: c. Howie Kendrick.

214: c. Anthony Rendon/Juan Soto.

215: a. Anibal Sanchez.

216: a. Juan Soto.

217: a. 8-0 (Strasburg 5-0, Scherzer 3-0).

218: b. Ryan Zimmerman.

219: c. Juan Soto (six runs, nine hits, three home runs; he also had seven RBIs, one fewer than Anthony Rendon).

220: d. Sean Doolittle.

TUCKER ELLIOT

ABOUT THE AUTHOR

Tucker Elliot is a former teacher, coach, and athletic director. He has visited schools on four continents and more than twenty countries as a volunteer or an invited speaker/lecturer. He lives in Florida and Korea.

e-Books by Tucker Elliot

The Day Before 9/11

The Memory of Hope

The Rainy Season

Third Ring Children

The Other Side of the River

Baseball Books by Tucker Elliot

Los Angeles Dodgers IQ: The Ultimate Test of True Fandom

Baltimore Orioles IQ: The Ultimate Test of True Fandom

Cincinnati Reds IQ: The Ultimate Test of True Fandom

Major League Baseball IQ: The Ultimate Test of True Fandom

Tampa Bay Rays IQ: The Ultimate Test of True Fandom

Atlanta Braves IQ: The Ultimate Test of True Fandom

Cleveland Indians IQ: The Ultimate Test of True Fandom

New York Yankees IQ: The Ultimate Test of True Fandom

San Francisco Giants IQ: The Ultimate Test of True Fandom

Houston Astros IQ: The Ultimate Test of True Fandom

Atlanta Braves: An Interactive Guide to the World of Sports

Boston Red Sox: An Interactive Guide to the World of Sports

San Francisco Giants: An Interactive Guide to the World of Sports

51 Questions for the Diehard Fan: New York Yankees

51 Questions for the Diehard Fan: Atlanta Braves

51 Questions for the Diehard Fan: Baltimore Orioles

BLACK MESA

Visit us on the web to learn more:

www.blackmesabooks.com

SOURCES

Baseball-reference.com (Play Index)

MLB.com (and the official team sites through MLB.com)

BaseballHallofFame.org

ESPN.com

SABR.org

Baseball-Almanac.com

Elias Sports Bureau

Black Mesa